GOD'S BLUE EARTH

GOD'S BLUE EARTH

Teaching Kids to Celebrate the Sacred Gift of Water

SUZANNE BLOKLAND
RANDY HAMMER

THE PILGRIM PRESS

CLEVELAND

The Pilgrim Press, 700 Prospect Avenue, Cleveland, Ohio 44122
thepilgrimpress.com
© 2013 by Suzanne Blokland and Randy Hammer

Printed in the United States of America on acid-free paper

17   16   15   14   13   5   4   3   2   1

Library of Congress Cataloging-in-Publication Data

Blokland, Suzanne, 1965–
    God's blue earth : teaching kids to celebrate the sacred gift of water / Suzanne Blokland,
    Randy Hammer.
        pages cm
    ISBN 978-0-8298-1941-0 (alk. paper)
    1. Water—Religious aspects—Christianity—Juvenile literature.   2. Water in the Bible.
I. Hammer, Randy, 1955–   II. Title.
BL450.B56 2013
261.8'8—dc23   2012044616

CONTENTS

Introduction

HOW TO USE THIS RESOURCE

God's Blue Earth can be considered a sequel to our earlier work, *What's So Amazing about Polar Bears? Teaching Kids to Care for Creation*, or it can stand on its own. Like its predecessor, *God's Blue Earth* is an interactive, Christian-based resource containing six lessons that can be used for Sunday school, Sunday evening gatherings, mid-week activities, vacation Bible school, or outdoor camp settings.

Each lesson focuses on water, with a Bible story related to water for study, reflection, and discussion; large and small group activities that utilize hands-on activities to engage the children and reinforce the Bible, cultural, and science lessons; fun facts relevant to the topic; story options; suggested music; lists of supplies needed; and a concluding prayer. The appendix has a sample letter to parents for each lesson, to share what the children have learned and offer suggestions for continuing this learning at home. This resource will encourage children to discover, experience, create, appreciate, respect, and help protect the sacred gift of water upon which all life on earth depends.

Each lesson contains a wealth of information and options from which the adult leader may draw to suit the needs of his or her particular situation. Generally speaking, the lessons begin with opening whole group activities that explore facts about water, proceed to traditional Bible stories and discussions, move on to small group activities that incorporate arts and crafts as well as science experiences, and reconvene for a whole group time that focuses on the water challenges children face in other countries, and finally conclude with a prayer. Most of the material is suitable for use both indoors and out, and leaders may pick and choose the activities that best suit their situation, time frame, and resources. One could spend multiple weeks of short sessions from each lesson, or focus on one lesson each day, as in the case of VBS or day-long camp settings. What makes this work unique is the integration of traditional Bible study with science and the experiential nature of the activities.

This resource has been designed especially for the interests and abilities of elementary children, but activities have been included to engage children as young as three years, for VBS and similar settings. Children may be assigned to small groups that experience the activities and lessons together. We would also encourage you to consider a less structured format, in which children are allowed to explore the activities individually and find what engages them most.

HELPFUL TIPS

About the Literature

The whole group activities incorporate the book *Our World of Water: Children and Water Around the World* by Beatrice Hollyer. In addition, each lesson suggests a children's book for story time. If your public library does not have these books, ask the librarian about securing them through interlibrary loan or for suggestions of alternate titles.

About the Activities

Depending on your situation, you may have children in a wide range of developmental stages and with a variety of learning styles. While some children may be able to sit and do crafts, others may need to move. Try to incorporate at least one activity that involves movement from each lesson. General precautions: Always use child-safe scissors, and exercise caution when children are using them, and, unless otherwise specified, use washable school glue. In addition, exercise care when children are around water.

Best wishes as you and your children study, explore, and celebrate the sacred gift of water!

ONE

Water in the Creation Story

SCRIPTURE TEXT
Genesis 1:1–2:4 (selected verses)

VERSE OF THE DAY
The Spirit of God was moving over the water. (Genesis 1:2 GNT)

PURPOSE OF THE LESSON
To explore and gain a greater appreciation for how water
is the origin of and vital to all life on the earth

FOR THE LEADER—AN OPENING MEDITATION

Water. Its importance on this earth is reflected by the mention of it in the second verse of the Bible. The "raging ocean" covered everything. "The Spirit of God was moving over the water." Scientists tell us that all life on this earth originated in water from tiny one-celled organisms and developed from there. I have long been fascinated by the way the King James Version of the Bible translates verse 20 of the first chapter of Genesis: "And God said, Let the waters bring forth abundantly the moving creature that hath life, and fowl that may fly above the earth in the open firmament of heaven." It is almost as if the KJV translators knew that all life originated in the sea. Apart from water, we would not be here.

So what a great gift is water, to be respected, appreciated, and celebrated. This is what we aim to do in the course of this study. We hope to assist our children, as well as adult leaders, in gaining a greater appreciation for water and the vital role it plays in the life of our planet.

From the raging oceans to the lazy rivers to the tranquil lakes to the bubbling mountain streams to the village wells that are the life source for many of our world, we celebrate the miracle of water and offer a prayer of gratitude for this wondrous gift.

Materials

- several sheets of green poster board
- roll of green paper
- blue copy or construction paper
- masking tape
- scissors
- atlas or map of the continents
- banner paper or poster board
- colorful copy paper (optional)
- colorful markers
- yarn
- toilet paper tube

Advanced Preparations

Draw the continents on the green poster board and cut them out. Make them large enough for children to see easily. Don't worry about every nook and cranny; just get the basic shape of each continent. Don't label the continents or mount them to the wall yet.

Make labels with the names of the continents, the United States, and two of your hometown.

Cut green paper from the roll into five-foot strips and tape them together to make a five-foot square. Cut a large circle from this square. Tape it to the wall where the children will gather for large group time.

Next, you'll need to cut the blue paper into large raindrops (about two drops per sheet) to cover 70 percent of the green circle. Don't worry about mathematical precision, as you just want to give children the basic idea. Lay the raindrops on the circle and eyeball it. Go for a little less than three-quarters of the circle. Put the raindrops and tape in a container near the circle taped to the wall.

Use the banner paper to make banners with the following declarations:

- God's Blue Earth: Celebrating the Sacred Gift of Water
- "The Spirit of God was moving over the water." (Genesis 1:2 GNT)
- The rainbow is the sign of God's covenant. (Genesis 9:13)
- Water is God's sacred gift to the world.
- "As Jesus was baptized . . . he saw the Spirit of God coming down like a dove and lighting on him." (Matthew 3:16 GNT)
- Jesus "ordered . . . the waves to stop, and there was a great calm." (Matthew 8:26 GNT)
- Wells provide life-giving water.

You can use the markers or cut letters from the colorful copy paper.

Do an Internet search to find out the annual rainfall for your hometown. Cut a piece of yarn to this length and wrap it around a toilet paper tube.

GATHERING TIME

Welcome the children. Ask them what the title of the study is (God's Blue Earth: Celebrating the Sacred Gift of Water). Say, "This week we'll be learning about what?" (water) "Let's start with a great song about water."

Gathering Music

"Itsy, Bitsy Raindrops" (Words by Dot Keller; tune: "Itsy, Bitsy Spider")

Itsy-bitsy raindrops are falling all around.
On the streets and sidewalks and on the sun-baked ground.
Making green our flowers and quenching thirsty trees.
Itsy, bitsy raindrops are falling down on me.

Or sing "I Sing the Mighty Power of God" (*The New Century Hymnal* #12).

WHOLE GROUP ACTIVITY
How Much of the Earth Is Covered in Water?

Purpose

To demonstrate to the children how much of the Earth is covered by water

Materials

- large, green circle
- blue raindrops
- tape

Procedure

Show the children the large circle. Say, "This circle represents our planet, Earth. The green stands for all the dry land. However, some of the Earth is covered with water. We're going to cover up the circle with paper raindrops to find out just how much is land and how much is water."

Let the children come up one or two at a time to tape raindrops on the circle. The raindrops should not overlap. To speed this up, let a helper or two distribute raindrops and tape to the kids who are waiting for their turn.

After the children are finished with the raindrops, step back and look at how much of the green has been covered up. Tell them, "Seventy percent, nearly three quarters, of the Earth is covered with water."

Tell the children that this week, as we learn about water, we'll share together some stories from the Bible that have water in them; we'll learn about children in other parts of the world and how they get and use water; and we'll explore some cool stuff about water itself.

FUN FACT: THE PACIFIC OCEAN COVERS 30 PERCENT OF THE EARTH'S SURFACE, MORE SURFACE AREA THAN ALL THE CONTINENTS PUT TOGETHER.

STUDYING

Verse of the Day

"The Spirit of God was moving over the water." (Genesis 1:2 GNT)

Bible Story: Genesis 1:1–2:4 (GNT)

In the beginning, when God created the universe, the earth was formless and desolate. The raging ocean that covered everything was engulfed in total darkness, and the Spirit of God was moving over the water. Then God commanded, "Let there be light"—and light appeared. Then he separated the light from the darkness, and he named the light "Day" and the darkness "Night." . . .

Then God commanded, "Let there be a dome to divide the water and to keep it in two separate places"—and it was done. . . . He named the dome "Sky." . . . Then God commanded, "Let the water below the sky come together in one place, so that the land will appear"—and it was done. He named the land "Earth," and the water which had come together he named "Sea." . . .

Then he commanded, "Let the earth produce all kinds of plants, those that bear grain and those that bear fruit"—and it was done. . . . Then God commanded, "Let lights appear in the sky to separate day from night and to show the time when days, years, and religious festivals begin; they will shine in the sky to give light to the earth"—and it was done. So God made the two larger lights, the sun to rule over the day and the moon to rule over the night; he also made the stars. . . . Then God commanded, "Let the water be filled with many kinds of living beings, and let the air be filled with birds." So God created the great sea monsters, all kinds of creatures that live in the water, and all kinds of birds. . . . Then God commanded, "Let the earth produce all kinds of animal life; domestic and wild, large and small"—and it was done. . . .

Then God said, "And now we will make human beings; they will be like us and resemble us. They will have power over the fish, the birds, and all animals, domestic and wild, large and small." So God created human beings, making them to be like himself. He created them male and female, blessed them, and said, "Have many children. . . ."

And so the whole universe was completed. By the seventh day God finished what he had been doing and stopped working. He blessed the seventh day and set it apart as a special day, because by that day he had completed his creation and stopped working. And that is how the universe was created.

Note: Consider downloading photographs of the earth, sun, moon, and stars taken from space and burning a DVD set to music to accompany the reading of today's scripture text.

Question and Discussion Time

Note: Some questions in the discussion time are open-ended. Use these as an opportunity for children to share and explore ideas. If the answers in parentheses are not mentioned, you can contribute them to the pool of ideas.

1. What is the first thing on earth that is mentioned in the creation story? (water, raging ocean)

2. Why do you think it is so important that water is the first thing mentioned in the creation story? (All life on earth originated from water.)

3. When the waters came together so that the land appeared, what were the big bodies of water called? (seas)

4. Can you name something found in water that is vital to human life on earth? (fish—for many people of the world their primary diet; salt)

5. Why is it so important that we celebrate and respect water? (Water is necessary for life; all life is dependent upon water.)

EXPLORING—SMALL GROUP ACTIVITIES

Note: Decide how you want to handle small group time. You can let children choose their own activities and stay with each one as long as interest holds them. Or you can put children into groups and have them rotate on a schedule. If you have a large group, you may prefer more structure. Before the children break into small groups, briefly describe the activities.

ACTIVITY ONE: Mural of Creation

Purpose

To reinforce the Bible story

Materials

- banner paper
- copy paper
- scissors
- paints
- disposable cups or bowls
- paintbrushes, various sizes
- marker
- tape or clamps
- smocks
- water
- scotch tape or glue sticks
- newspapers

Preparation

Draw broad outlines on banner paper of sky, water, and land. Use tape or clamps to attach the paper to a vertical surface. If you are indoors, be sure you cover the floor with newspapers. If you prefer, the children can work with the paper on the ground, but be careful that they don't walk over it too much.

Procedure

Note: This activity can be divided into two parts, worked on simultaneously. Painting in the mural background of sky, earth, and sea is good for children who need to move or don't have the patience for detail work. Painting images to go on the background is good for children who prefer detail work.

Give each child a smock. If children want to paint the mural background, give them a cup or bowl of blue, green, or brown paint and a large brush. Show them where each color should go. You may want to use two colors of blue, one for the sky and one for the sea.

Other children can paint pictures to go on the background. Give them a sheet of copy paper, access to various colors of paint, and brushes. Make sure they have cups of water to clean brushes before switching paint colors. You may need to monitor this with

young children. Alternately, you could put a brush in each paint cup, to be used only with that color.

Tell them to paint a picture of something mentioned in the Bible story. Ideas include the sun, moon, stars, plants, sea animals, land animals, birds, fruits, vegetables, and people. Don't worry if everyone wants to paint a sun.

Once a child has painted a picture, it can be cut out and glued or taped to the mural background, after the background has dried.

ACTIVITY TWO: Save the Egg Family's Beach Vacation! Saltwater Versus Freshwater

Purpose

To discover that adding salt to water makes it easier for things to float

Materials

- one raw egg per child and extras
- hand sanitizer
- permanent markers
- clear plastic bowls or glasses
- pitcher
- bucket of water
- salt (See "Notes" below.)
- measuring spoons
- spoons
- sand (optional)
- tray (optional)
- cooler (optional)

Notes: You can use ordinary table salt for this activity, just keep in mind that the additives in the salt will make the water murky. For clearer water, use natural sea salt with no additives. (The ingredient list will list only sea salt.)

For testing purposes, we used a bowl that holds three cups of water and found that two tablespoons of salt per cup of water buoyed the egg.

Preparation

Spread the sand on a tray, to make a beach for your eggs.

Prop the eggs in the sand and have the other supplies at hand. (Optional: To make sure your eggs stay fresh, keep most of them in a cooler and put a few on the sand at a time.)

Fill several bowls or glasses with fresh (unsalted) water.

Procedure

As the children come to the station, give them each an egg and a permanent marker. Ask them to draw a face on the egg. They can add a bathing suit if they like.

While the children are decorating their eggs, ask if they've ever been to the beach. What did they notice about the water? (It's salty.) Did they also notice that they found it easier to float in the ocean than in the swimming pool? That's because all that salt in the water makes it easier for us to float.

Tell the children that the Egg family has come to the beach, but they are very disappointed. Every time they try to swim in the ocean, they sink right to the bottom.

Give each child a glass or a bowl with water. Have them set their eggs in the containers. (*Note:* Make sure the water is deep enough to completely submerge the egg.)

Explain that then the Egg family realized there was no salt in the ocean! Have the children remove their eggs, then stir salt into the water, one tablespoon at a time, until their eggs float.

Say, "You've saved the Egg family's beach vacation! You're a hero!"

Have children clean their hands with sanitizer after they finish this activity.

ACTIVITY THREE: It Rained HOW Much?!—Making Rain Gauges

Purpose

To make a rain gauge and learn how they are used

Materials

- clear, plastic bottles (See "Note.")
- small gravel or sand
- duct tape
- dark permanent markers

- colorful permanent markers
- rulers
- knife
- table
- plastic grocery bags
- instructions (See "Preparation" below.)
- sandwich-size zip style baggies (optional)

Note: Bottles with straight, smooth sides are most accurate, but hard to find. Use what you have available, but avoid bottles that curve in a lot. Bottles need to be at least the sixteen-ounce size.

Preparation

Cut off the top of the bottles about one third of the way down from the top and keep both parts. Make sure there are no jagged edges.

Make copies of these instructions, to be sent home with the rain gauge:

- When rain is predicted, add gravel/sand and water to your rain gauge up to the baseline.
- Place the gauge in an open area, away from buildings and anything that might obstruct rainfall. Try to avoid windy areas.
- After the rain, read your gauge.

Procedure

Give each child a bottle and the colorful markers. Let them decorate the bottom part of the bottle on one side. They will need to leave the other side clear in order to add the measurements.

Fill the bottom of the bottle with gravel or sand, up to the point where the sides straighten. This stabilizes the bottle and improves accuracy in measuring. You may need to tap the bottle to level the gravel/sand.

Slowly pour water into the bottle until it reaches the top of the gravel/sand. Wait until the water stops moving, then mark the top of the water level with a line, using a dark marker. Put the number "0" at this line. (Water can be emptied out at this point.)

Help the children hold a ruler at the "0" mark and mark off inches and quarter inches with the dark marker, using longer lines for the inches and shorter lines for the quarter inches. If you find it easier, empty the gravel/sand into a baggie to be taken home. Then the children can lay the bottles on their sides for marking.

Number the inch lines.

Turn the top of the bottle (that was cut off) upside down and fit it into the bottom. Tape the edges together.

Place the rain gauge, baggie of gravel/sand (if applicable), and instructions in a plastic grocery bag and label it with child's name.

ACTIVITY FOUR: Water Is Sticky

Purpose

To introduce children to the cohesive property of water

Materials

- plastic cups
- bucket of water
- ladle
- dropper
- tape (any kind)
- uncooked rice

Procedure

As children come to your station, give each one a few grains of rice and a piece of tape. Let them lay the rice on the table and use the tape to pick it up. Ask them why the tape could pick up the rice. (It's sticky.) Ask the children, "Did you know that water is sticky, too?"

Tell them that water molecules (the tiniest pieces of water) like each other and tend to stick together.

Give each child a plastic cup. Using the ladle, the child can fill the cup level with the brim (but not over). Then, using the dropper, the child can add water drops, noting that the water will bulge up over the brim for a while before gravity finally pulls it down. The water is able to bulge like this because it sticks together.

ACTIVITY FIVE: Geographical Features

Purpose

To introduce children to the following geographical features: lake, island, peninsula, strait, isthmus, and gulf

Materials

- poster board
- green modeling clay (do not use play dough)
- pitcher
- bucket of water
- small containers, any shape, approximately six inches in diameter
- black permanent marker
- blue marker or crayon
- green marker or crayon
- ruler

Preparation

Use the sharpie to divide the poster board into six squares.

In each square, use simple shapes to draw each geographical feature. Add definitions if you'll be working with older children. Suggestions are as follow:

Gulf: A gulf is a large area of sea or ocean that is partially enclosed by land. Draw a semicircle at the bottom of the square. Color the semicircle blue and the rest of the square green.

Island: An island is a tract of land that is surrounded by a river, lake, or the ocean. It is smaller than a continent. Draw a circle in the middle of the square and color it green. Color the rest of the square blue.

Isthmus: An isthmus is a narrow strip of land that joins two large areas of land and narrowly separates two large bodies of water. Draw two large circles in the square and connect them with a narrow rectangle. Color the circles and rectangle green and the rest blue.

Lake: A lake is a body of water surrounded by land. Draw a circle in the middle of the square and color it blue. Color the rest green.

Peninsula: A peninsula is a stretch of land that juts out into an ocean or lake and is almost completely surrounded by water. Draw an oval at the top of the square and another skinny oval connected to it. Color the ovals green and the rest blue.

Strait: A strait is a narrow waterway connecting two large bodies of water. Draw two ovals close to each other but not touching. Color the ovals green and the rest blue.

Procedure

Give each child some modeling clay and a container. Show them the poster board with the various geographical features. Encourage them to pick one and make it in their container, using the green clay to match the green on the poster board. The blue stands for the water, which is poured into the container after the clay is in place. (Remember to use modeling clay, which will not get soggy in water.)

If they like, they can pour the water out and make another feature.

ACTIVITY SIX: Stained Glass Creation Scenes

Purpose

To help children recall details from the Bible story

Materials

- crayons
- old grater or old blender
- black construction paper
- wax paper
- tape
- iron
- heavy cardboard or ironing board
- cardboard from cereal boxes
- scissors
- pencils
- zip style baggies

Preparation

Note: We recommend practicing this ahead of time to get an idea of how many crayon shavings are needed for a translucent effect. A little goes a long way.

Shave a variety of colors of crayons. You can use an old grater, if you have one, or a blender that you don't need any more. Store the colors in separate zip style baggies.

Cut black construction paper into rectangles. A good size is approximately 4.5 inches by 5.5 inches.

Cut stencils from cereal box cardboard. Stencils should correspond to the creation story and can include sun, moon, stars, animals, fish, foods, or people. Keep the designs simple and small enough to fit on the black paper.

Procedure

Note: You will need to be close to an outlet to plug in the iron. The iron should be attended at all times by an adult and used only by an adult.

Have children choose a stencil and trace it onto the black paper and cut it out.

Tear off a piece of wax paper about twice as big as the black paper. Place the black paper over one half of the wax paper.

Children can sprinkle crayon shavings through the black paper cut out onto the wax paper.

Carefully remove the black paper and fold the other half of the wax paper over the crayon shavings.

Very carefully, move the wax paper to the ironing board and iron it. (You may want to practice ahead of time to get the hang of it.)

Once the crayon has melted and briefly cooled, let child tape the wax paper to the back of the black paper so that the melted crayon shows through the cut out. Hang it in a window.

ACTIVITY SEVEN: What Dissolves in Water?

Purpose

To introduce children to the idea that water will dissolve a lot of things

Materials

- bucket of water
- three-ounce paper cups
- spoons
- sand
- sugar
- salt
- rocks
- lemonade mix
- antacid tablets

Procedure

Ask the children if they know what dissolve means? Tell them that if you dissolve something, you put it in a liquid and it becomes part of the liquid. You can't see it anymore. This activity is going to let the children explore different solids to find which will dissolve.

Children can choose any number of solids to try. For each solid, give them a three-ounce cup with water. Using the spoon, they can add a little solid to the water and stir. What happens? Do all the solids turn to liquid?

You can point out to the children that water will dissolve (turn to liquid) more things than any other liquid. This is one reason why we need water in our bodies, to help dissolve the foods we eat so our bodies can use them.

ACTIVITY EIGHT: Soup Ladle Relay

Purpose

To move water from one bucket to another, using a soup ladle

Note: Relays can be set up as an activity, with children participating as they wish, or it can be used to bring the whole group back together at the end of small group time.

Materials

- two buckets per team
- one soup ladle per team
- popcorn or packaging peanuts, if indoors

Preparation

Find a suitable place for the relay, such as a grassy area. If you need to move indoors, use the popcorn (popped) or packaging peanuts instead of water.

Place a bucket at each end of the relay course for each team. Fill the buckets at one end with water.

Procedure

Emphasize to the children that the point of relays is to have fun. They aren't to worry about winning and losing.

Divide the children into two teams and line them up at one end. Give the first child on each team a soup ladle.

Tell the children that the object of the relay is to move water from one bucket to the other, using the ladle. On "Go," the first child scoops water into the ladle, walks/runs to the other end, empties the water into the bucket, then runs back and passes the ladle to the next child in line.

Continue until one team runs out of water. The winning team is the team with the most water in the second bucket.

REGROUPING—STORY TIME

Use story time to transition from the busy small group time to the more structured whole group time. This gives the children a chance to settle down and focus on what the leader is saying.

Book

Splish, Splash, poems by Joan Bransfield Graham, illustrated by Steve Scott (New York: Tickner & Fields, 1994).

WHOLE GROUP ACTIVITIES

ACTIVITY ONE: Discussing the Country of the Day—United States

Purpose

To help children begin to think about how they get and use water, which they will later compare to methods used by people in other countries

Materials

- large sheets of paper, which can be cut into raindrop shapes
- marker
- masking tape

Preparation

Write the following questions, either on the sheets of paper or on index cards:

- What do you use water for? (Answers can include everyday activities and special activities, such as swimming.)
- How do you get water? Hot water? How many faucets are in your house?
- Is your water clean?
- Do you have to be careful with how much water you use? Do you take baths? How often? With warm or cold water?

Procedure

Encourage children to start thinking and sharing ideas. Sometimes you may not see the logic in their answers until you understand how they arrived there. Try to use all the answers you can.

Tape the first sheet on the wall and ask the children the first question. Give them time to discuss as you write their answers on the sheet.

Continue with each sheet.

Ask the children why humans need water. Do they think it is important for people to be able to get clean water?

CONSERVATION TIP: ACCORDING TO THE EPA, THE AVERAGE AMERICAN FAMILY OF FOUR USES 400 GALLONS OF WATER EVERY DAY, 280 OF THOSE GALLONS INDOORS.

ACTIVITY TWO: Hanging up the Continents

Purpose

To display the map that you'll be using for these lessons and to help children learn the shapes and relative locations of the continents.

Materials (See "Advanced Preparations" at beginning of lesson.)

- cut-out of continents
- labels with continent names
- masking tape

Procedure

Ask children if they know what a continent is (the largest land masses on our planet). Begin with North America. Hold up the cutout of the continent and ask children if they know which one it is. Once they've named it (with your help, if necessary), tape it to the wall. You can enlist a child to help you.

One at a time, hold up the rest of the continents, name them, and tape them approximately where they should go in relation to the others. Again, allow children to help and don't worry about absolute accuracy. Children are just getting a general feel for where the continents are.

As a review of what you've just done, hold up the labels and let the children point out which label goes on which land mass. Tape them to the appropriate place.

ACTIVITY THREE: Annual Rainfall

Purpose

To introduce the practice of measuring rainfall and to compare annual rainfall in different locations

Materials (See "Advanced Preparations" at beginning of lesson.)

- labels with name of your hometown and the United States
- yarn showing annual rainfall in your hometown

Procedure

Ask the children if they made rain gauges. Can anyone explain how they work? (When it rains, set the gauge out and after the rain, measure how much rain fell by checking the measurements on the side.) Tell children that scientists are always measuring rainfall with rain gauges. They can tell us how much rain falls in different places in a whole year. One of the things we're going to do in each lesson is learn how much rain falls every year in different places on the Earth.

Today, we're going to start with our hometown. (If you have small children, ask what the name of your town is.) First, what country is our town located in? (Place the label of the United States on the map.) Now, does anyone know where our town is? (Place that label on the map.) Can you guess how much rain we get every year? (Children can guess by giving measurements, such as ten inches, or by standing and showing how much they think.)

Our town gets [insert statistic of your town's annual rainfall] inches of rain each year. Let's see how much that is. (Invite a child to help you unroll the yarn and tape it to the wall. Attach the label with the name of your hometown.)

Tell the children that tomorrow, they'll learn about the rainfall in another place.

CLOSING

Reviewing

- What new thing did you learn today?
- What was important about the exploring activities (naming specific activities from the available suggestions that were implemented) that you participated in?
- Of all the things that you did and learned today, which one excites you most?

PARTING PRAYER

O God, we express our thanks for the wonderful gift of water and all the life it makes possible for our world. Be with us throughout this week as we learn more about water and how important it is to children all around the world. Amen.

TWO

Noah and the Flood

SCRIPTURE TEXT
Genesis 6:9–9:16 (selected verses)

VERSE OF THE DAY
The rainbow is the sign of God's covenant. (Genesis 9:13)

PURPOSE OF THE LESSON
*To celebrate the rainbow as a sign of God's promise and
to learn about the water cycle*

FOR THE LEADER—AN OPENING MEDITATION

The fact that a number of ancient cultures passed on sacred myths about a massive flood that covered the entire earth makes us want to believe that there was indeed a time (or perhaps more than one time) when that part of the world where each story originated did indeed experience a massive flood that would have appeared to have covered the entire earth. With the recent floods at different locations around world, such an idea does not seem so far-fetched.

And in the ancient view of things, such natural disasters naturally were attributed to God, or the gods, as punishment upon wicked humanity. There may be some today who still hold such views. But those of us who hold a more progressive faith generally do not attribute such natural events to an angry God. Such, we understand, is the way of the universe and the natural order of things.

So we believe it is important when sharing the story of Noah and the flood with children that we be careful about the way we do so. We believe that it is desirable to pass on this important story to our children, as it is a vital piece of world religious history and literature. But rather than focusing on the wickedness of humanity and God's regret over having created humans, we prefer to focus on God's covenant of promise.

Yes, floods happen. They have always happened. We understand today how storm clouds form and pour down the rain that causes tiny streams to become raging rivers and lakes that can cover homes. We can instill in our children a healthy respect for water's destructive possibilities. But we can also emphasize a loving God who is saddened when floods adversely affect people's lives. We can share news of a God who doesn't send suffering, but who suffers with those who suffer. We can teach our children that the rainbow they see in the sky following the rain is there to remind us that God cares for us and makes promises to us because God loves us.

Materials

- corrugated box
- duct tape (brown, if you have it)
- brown paint
- paintbrush
- poster board
- colored markers

Advanced Preparations

First, build an ark. Use the biblical dimensions of 450 feet long by 75 feet wide by 45 feet high as a guide (for scale—of course, your ark will be much smaller!). Use whatever building material you have readily available—a corrugated box will work well. Don't get too bent out of shape about exact dimensions or whether your end product actually looks like a boat. The kids will get the general idea that the ark was intended to be quite long and narrow. If you have a piece of cardboard big enough, make the length about 45 inches, the width about 7.5 inches, and the height about 4.5 inches. If you need a different size ark, adjust the measurements accordingly. One of the activities for this lesson has children making animals for the ark. Think about how large the animals will be as you decide how large to build the ark.

Next, make a laundry cycle poster. To help children understand the concept of a cycle, make a funny poster about the laundry cycle. Using simple stick figures, at the top of the poster draw a happy person with clean clothes. Draw an arrow pointing toward the right side of the poster. On the right side, draw the same person with dirty clothes and a sad face. Draw an arrow pointing toward the bottom of the poster. On the bottom, draw a washing machine and an arrow pointing to the left side. On the left side, draw the clothes hanging on a line to dry and an arrow pointing toward the top.

GATHERING TIME

Welcome the children. Tell them you're glad to see them again. Ask what they remember about the last session. (Possible responses include how much water is on the Earth, the Bible story, the small group activities, and how much rain your town gets.)

Say, "Today we're going to explore more about water, hear a Bible story about how water once covered the earth, and learn what it's like to live in a country called Bangladesh, where there are a lot of floods."

"Let's start with our water song, 'Itsy Bitsy Raindrops.'" (Or use the alternate hymn.)

Gathering Music

"Itsy, Bitsy Raindrops" (Words by Dot Keller; tune: "Itsy, Bitsy Spider")

Itsy-bitsy raindrops are falling all around.
On the streets and sidewalks and on the sun-baked ground.
Making green our flowers and quenching thirsty trees.
Itsy, bitsy raindrops are falling down on me.

Or sing "God Reigns o'er All the Earth" (*The New Century Hymnal* #21, verse 1).

WHOLE GROUP ACTIVITY
The Water Cycle

Purpose

To introduce the concept of the water cycle

Materials

- laundry cycle poster
- electric griddle
- extension cord
- ice cubes
- clean glass bowl
- freshwater
- salt
- spoon

Procedure

Explain the laundry cycle poster to give children an idea that a cycle is never ending. Point to the person at the top and explain that this is a happy person with clean clothes. Point to the person on the right side and ask children what this is (a sad person with dirty clothes). Point to the bottom and ask what this is (a washing machine). What does it do? (It cleans clothes.) Point to the left and ask what this is (clothes hanging to dry). Finally, point to the top again and ask what this is. You can circle the poster a couple of times to help the kids understand the cycle, clean to dirty to clean again. Make this fun. Ask an adult (especially a mom) if the laundry cycle ever ends. (Never!)

Nature has cycles, too. Ask children if they know of any cycles in nature. (Examples include the rock cycle, life cycle, carbon cycle, and water cycle.) Tell the children that today we're going to look at the water cycle. Ask, "Now in the laundry cycle, it was your laundry that was moving around in a circle. What is moving around in the water cycle?"

Demonstrate the water cycle. As you go through the activity, introduce vocabulary: evaporation, condensation, precipitation (last two in Activity 9 below). Also talk about the different forms water can take: solid, liquid, and gas.

Say, "I have a griddle here. We use this to make pancakes at my house. It has a cord that plugs into the wall. Before I plug it into the wall, let's talk about how to be safe with this griddle." (Let kids give ideas, but make sure they understand they are not to use the plug or touch the hot griddle.)

Okay, I'm going to plug it in and what will happen? (It will heat up.) The griddle represents the sun because it gives off heat.

(Take out one ice cube.) Say, "I have this ice cube. This is going to be snow. Snow is frozen water and ice is frozen water. What will happen when I put this ice cube on the hot griddle?" (Put ice on griddle.)

As the ice melts, it turns first to liquid water, then to steam, which rises from griddle. (CAUTION: Never put hand over steam.) Point out to the kids the different forms of water (ice, liquid, gas/water vapor). (Note to adults, but not necessarily for kids: the steam you can actually see is not water vapor, but rather tiny water droplets. Water vapor is invisible. In fact, when scientists talk about steam, they mean the water vapor, but the common usage of the word means this fog-like stuff. If you see steam from a tea kettle, note that it is invisible right at the spout—this is true water vapor.)

Ask kids, "Where is the steam going?" (up)

Repeat the activity, but this time put a glass bowl over the ice cube so the children can see the water droplets collecting on the bowl. Help the children notice that the water is collecting on the bowl and turning back into water drops, which are dripping down the bowl, back to the griddle. Perhaps you can get them to think about what happens to the water drops that drip back to the hot griddle. Maybe they can begin to see that the process can repeat itself indefinitely.

Ask, "Why is it helpful that water goes through this cycle? One reason is to get the salt out of it. Remember when we talked about all the water on Earth? Where is most of the water?" (oceans) "Can we drink it?" (no) "Why not?" (salty) "But when the water evaporates, it leaves the salt behind and the water becomes freshwater. Let's go back to our griddle and see how this happens."

Pour salt into a cup and add water. Stir till salt dissolves, then scoop a bit of water onto the griddle and let the water evaporate.

After the water is gone, there will be white stuff on the griddle. Ask the kids what they think this is. (salt)

Recap the lesson. Say, "So you know that the sun warms up the water and changes it into water vapor. Then it rises into the air, where it gets cooler. What happens to the water vapor then?" (It condenses.) "The water then comes back to Earth. We call that precipitation. What are some kinds of precipitation?" (snow, hail, rain) "Now we're going to hear a story from the Bible about a whole lot of precipitation."

STUDYING

Focus of the Day

The rainbow is the sign of God's covenant. (Genesis 9:13, GNT)

Bible Story: Genesis 6:9–9:16 (selected verses, paraphrased)

A long, long time ago, there lived a good man whose name was Noah. Noah had three sons. And Noah was very careful to live as he thought God wanted him to live.

One day God told Noah to build a big boat, and to use the best lumber to do so. Then he was told to cover it outside with tar so it wouldn't leak. God told Noah that he was going to make an agreement with him. A day was coming when he was to take his wife, and his sons, and their wives into the boat. And he also was to take a male and a female of every kind of bird and animal on the earth into the boat with them. And they needed to take enough food into the boat for themselves and all the birds and animals as well! That was a lot of food, wasn't it?

Pretty soon it started to rain. And it rained for so many days, the earth started to flood. It rained constantly for forty days and forty nights. The water got deeper and deeper, and the boat started to float. Finally the whole earth was covered, even the mountains.

Finally it stopped raining and the water started to go down. Noah sent out a dove, but in no time it came back because there was no place for it to light. After seven more days, Noah sent the dove out again, and this time it returned with an olive branch in its beak. After seven more days, Noah sent the dove out again, but this time it never came back. It had found a new home in the trees. After many days, the water was gone and the earth started to get dry again.

So Noah and all his family went out of the boat, taking all the birds and animals with them. God told Noah and his family to have many children. God made an agreement with Noah, saying, "I will make sure that a flood will never again cover the entire earth. And here is the sign of my promise: After it rains, I will put a beautiful rainbow in the sky. It will be the sign of my promise to the world."

Question and Discussion Time

1. Why do you think Noah was the one who built the ark? (He was a good man, lived in fellowship with God, was wise and able to see what was going on in the world.)

2. What was important about the animals that were taken onto the ark? (male and female of each kind)

3. Do you think the story about Noah is the only ancient story about a big flood? (No, many cultures have similar flood stories.)

4. Why was it important that the dove that Noah sent out came back with an olive branch in its mouth? (It meant there was life on the earth again.)

5. What was the sign of God's promise that the earth would never again be totally destroyed by water, that we sometimes still see today? (rainbow)

EXPLORING—SMALL GROUP ACTIVITIES

ACTIVITY ONE: The Animals Came Two by Two

Purpose

To create animals to fill Noah's ark

Note: This is an open-ended activity that allows children to be creative. Don't worry if their creations don't match reality.

Materials (The following materials are suggestions—feel free to improvise.)

- ark made in "Advanced Preparations"
- toilet paper tubes
- pudding boxes
- craft foam sheets
- googly eyes
- construction paper
- scissors
- markers
- craft feathers
- tape

- tacky glue or school glue
- pipe cleaners
- craft paints
- paint brushes
- small, disposable drinking cups
- bowl of water
- cotton balls
- yarn
- felt
- homemade play dough (See recipe below.)
- smocks
- wipes

Preparation

Make play dough, using the following recipe: Mix two cups of flour, one cup of salt, and one tablespoon cream of tartar in a large pan. Add two cups of water, two tablespoons of oil, and food coloring, if desired. Stir well over medium heat with a wooden spoon until the mixture pulls together. Knead well and store in a large plastic bag.

Procedure

Show the children the materials and ask them to use them to create an animal for Noah's ark.

Suggest they use a toilet paper tube or pudding box for the body and the rest of the materials however they see fit.

ACTIVITY TWO: Make a Rainbow

Purpose

To recall the rainbow as a sign of God's covenant with people

Note: This is a good activity for small children, as it involves gluing small pieces of paper to poster board. Encourage all the children to take a few minutes to help fill out the rainbow.

Materials

- construction or tissue paper, the colors of the rainbow
- scissors or paper cutter
- glue/glue sticks
- poster board
- pencil
- marker
- baggies or small containers for each color of paper

Preparation

Use the scissors or paper cutter to cut the paper into small pieces between half an inch and one inch square. Separate the colors into baggies or small containers.

Use the pencil to sketch a rainbow outline on the poster board. Make as many arches as you have colors; don't worry if you don't have indigo.

Glue one piece of paper onto each arch so children know where to put the different colors. The top arch is red, then orange, yellow, green, blue, indigo, with violet at the bottom.

Procedure

Remind the children that the story of Noah tells us that the rainbow is a symbol of God's covenant or promise that the earth would never be totally destroyed by water.

Ask them to help make a rainbow to display over the ark by gluing pieces of paper onto the poster board.

ACTIVITY THREE: How Can a Big Boat Float?

Purpose

To explore the difference that shape makes in whether something can float

Materials

- container of water
- modeling clay
- dried beans

Preparation

Roll the clay into balls.

Procedure

When children arrive at this station, give each a ball of clay and tell them to put the clay in the water. What happens to the clay?

Now, challenge them to make the clay float. If they do not understand right away that they need to change the shape, you can guide them toward this idea, but let them experiment with shapes until they find one that works.

If they want, once they have a shape that floats, they can add beans to their boats to see how many the boats can hold before they sink.

Challenge them to make boats that can hold more beans.

ACTIVITY FOUR: What Floats? (especially for young children)

Purpose

To explore which objects float and which sink

Materials

- shallow tub of water
- a variety of small objects (Include objects of the same shape but different materials, such as ping pong balls and marbles, plastic spoons and metal spoons.)

Procedure

CAUTION: Always watch children around water.

As children come to the station, allow them to explore different objects to see what floats and what sinks. You can encourage them to predict before they put an object in the water.

Help them notice that objects that have the same shape can float or sink and explore with them the reason. (They're made of different materials.)

ACTIVITY FIVE: Build a Flood-proof Home

Purpose

To explore ways to live in flood-prone areas by building a home that can withstand floods

Note: This is an open-ended activity, giving children opportunity to use their imagination. Older children can be encouraged to sketch an idea and try to build it. Very young children may be content to decorate a shoebox to look like a house.

Materials

- shoeboxes
- toilet paper and paper towel rolls
- dowel rods (cut to about twelve inches)
- lots of tape
- paper and pencils to sketch ideas (for older kids)
- extras to make the house look cute—like scraps of fabric for curtains and rugs
- odds and ends to make furniture, such as pudding boxes
- styrofoam
- empty plastic water bottles
- scissors
- knife (for adult use only)

Procedure

Tell children, "People who live in Bangladesh have to live with flooding every year. One way they do this is by creating houses that can be taken apart and moved. Children also go to schools that float."

Ask, "What would you do if you lived in a place that flooded every year? Can you think of a way to build a house to keep you dry?"

Give each child a shoebox to turn into a house or school. They can draw windows and doors, which an adult can cut out, and add furniture, curtains, and rugs, if time permits.

Encourage the children to think about ways to keep their houses or schools dry in a flood. (Ideas could include building stilts with paper towel tubes under the boxes to elevate them, building a raft from dowel rods to set the box on, or building a pontoon from water bottles.)

ACTIVITY SIX: Water Cycle

Purpose

To set up an experiment that demonstrates the water cycle

Materials

- foam disposable bowls
- three-ounce paper cups
- rubber cement
- scissors
- rubber bands big enough to fit around the bowl
- tape
- plastic wrap
- small rocks
- pitcher of water

Preparation

For each child, you will need to prepare a bowl. Cut the paper cups down until they are shorter than the bowl.

Glue the bottom of the cups to the inside bottom of the bowls with the rubber cement. Let dry several hours or overnight.

Procedure

Give each child a bowl with the cup glued to the bottom. They need to pour water in the bowl, but not in the cup.

Next, instruct them to put plastic wrap over the top of the bowl. This will be tricky and may require two people. You need to stretch the wrap so that it lies flat, without folds and creases. Use the rubber band and the tape to secure the wrap. Double check that the wrap is smooth across the top and doesn't touch the cup.

Put a small rock right in the center of the plastic wrap, over the empty cup. The rock will weigh the plastic down and help you collect water in the cup. Again, the wrap should not touch the cup.

Leave bowl outside in the sun for a few hours, or even a whole day. The longer you leave it out, the more water you'll collect.

Tell the children that energy from the sun warms the water until it evaporates and becomes a gas. When the gas rises and hits the plastic wrap, it turns back into water drops. Eventually, gravity makes the water drops roll down the plastic wrap towards the rock. Then the water drops slide off the plastic wrap and into the glass, like rain. Water evaporates in the same way from lakes, rivers, and oceans. The water heats up, turns into a gas, and then condenses to fall back down as rain, snow, or hail.

ACTIVITY SEVEN: Building a Levee

Purpose

To explore one way to keep rising waters from flooding a community

Note: Small children will enjoy just playing with the sand and water. Allow them to do this, as long as others can do the activity.

Materials

- long, narrow plastic container, such as designed for under the bed
- play sand
- zip style sandwich baggies
- bucket
- water
- piece of 2x4 lumber, approximately the width of the container
- small plastic blocks to represent houses
- Frisbee or something similar

Advanced Preparation

Prop one narrow end of the container on the 2x4. Fill this end with sand, extending about one third of the way down.

Fill the rest of the container with water.

Procedure

Tell the children that people who live near water need ways to keep the water from flooding their homes. One way is to build a levee. Tell them they are going to build a levee with sand bags.

Give children baggies and let them fill them halfway with sand and zip them up. (This can be done ahead of time, if you prefer.)

Let the children build a village by placing the plastic blocks on the sand. Then they can build a wall with the sandbags to keep the water off the village. This is the levee.

Once the levee is in place, use the Frisbee to push the water toward the sand. Let the children see whether their levee keeps the rising waters off the village. They can make changes if necessary.

ACTIVITY EIGHT: Clouds

Purpose

To learn about the different kinds of clouds

Materials

- blue construction paper
- cotton balls
- quilt batting (optional)
- glue
- book about clouds, such as *The Cloud Book,* by Tomie de Paola (New York: Holiday House, 1975).
- crayons

Preparation

Using pictures from your book as a guide, sketch out the three basic types of clouds: cirrus, cumulus, and stratus. Cirrus is wispy, like feathers or horse tails; cumulus is puffy; and stratus is like a blanket. You often see nimbus combined with these types, such as cumulonimbus. Nimbus means a cloud that already has rain or snow falling from it.

Procedure

Young children may just be interested in gluing cotton balls on the paper.

Talk with children about what they learned about the water cycle. Ask what water vapor becomes when it goes into the sky (clouds). Show children the sketches you've made of the clouds or pictures from a book. Explain that there are three basic types of clouds: cirrus, cumulus, and stratus. Point out that the cirrus clouds look like feathers or a horse's tail when it is running. These clouds mean the weather will change soon. Point out that the cumulus clouds are puffy and look like cotton balls, and the stratus clouds look like a blanket across the sky.

Give each child access to the construction paper, cotton balls, batting (if using), and glue. Tell them to use these to make the different kinds of clouds. They can put them all on one sheet of paper or different sheets.

If they need guidance, show them how to pull the cotton balls and batting apart to resemble the cirrus and stratus clouds.

They can draw a picture to go with the clouds.

If there are clouds in your sky, look with the children to try to figure out which kind you see. It can be a bit tricky, as often the different types combine to form new types, but at least the children may begin to see that there is a difference between clouds.

ACTIVITY NINE: Rescue Animals from the Flood Relay

Purpose

To rescue "animals" caught in the flood and bring them to Noah's ark

Note: This is a wet activity, good for a hot day. If you are indoors or the weather is cooler, do the relay without water. If you are indoors on a slick floor, slow children down by making them do a crab walk, carrying the eggs on their stomachs.

Materials

- plastic eggs, or something similar that floats
- permanent markers
- four tubs
- water
- two empty plastic milk cartons, gallon or half gallon
- scissors
- nail or sharp knife

Preparation

Use the marker to draw animals on the plastic eggs.

Make a scoop by cutting away part of the milk cartons. Be sure to leave the handle intact. Then use the nail or knife to punch holes in the bottom of the milk cartons, so water can drain out.

Set two tubs at one end of the relay course and fill with water. Add the animal eggs. Set the other tubs at the opposite end.

Procedure

Divide the children into two groups and line them up at the end of the course with the empty tub.

Tell the children that the empty tubs are Noah's ark. Unfortunately, the animals are caught in the flood at the other end and need to be rescued.

Give the lead child on each team a scoop and tell them to scoop up one animal from their tub at the other end and bring it to the ark. The first team to bring all their animals on board wins.

REGROUPING — STORY TIME

Book: *Did a Dinosaur Drink This Water?* by Robert E. Wells (Park Ridge, IL: A. Whitman, 2006).

WHOLE GROUP ACTIVITIES

ACTIVITY ONE: Discussing the Country of the Day—Bangladesh

Purpose

To locate Bangladesh on the map and discover its annual rainfall

Materials

- strip of blue yarn cut to 100 inches (8 feet, 4 inches)
- paper towel tube
- rubber band
- two labels with Bangladesh written on them

Preparation

Roll the blue yarn onto a paper towel tube and secure with rubber band.

Procedure

After story time, draw children's attention to the world map that was assembled during Lesson One, "Water in the Creation Story." Remind them that yesterday they learned where their town was located and how much rain they got in one year. Tell them today they are going to look at another country, Bangladesh.

Show them the Bangladesh label and ask if anyone knows where it belongs. If no one knows, call on a child to help you attach it to the proper place.

Tell children that today they are going to learn about a boy named Saran, who lives in northern Bangladesh. Would anyone like to guess how much rain falls in his town? Allow the child who guesses closest to help you unroll the yarn. Attach the yarn next to the one from Lesson One and tape the second Bangladesh label to it.

ACTIVITY TWO: Comparing Our Lives

Purpose

To compare the children's daily lives with that of a boy who lives in Bangladesh

Materials

- seven small slips of paper
- bowl
- tape
- pen

Preparation

On the seven slips of paper, write questions 1–7 that appear under "Procedure." Do not write the responses about Saran. Fold the slips of paper and place them in the bowl.

Procedure

If you have the book *Our World of Water* by Beatrice Hollyer, show the children a picture of Saran.

Select children to draw the paper slips from the bowl and read the questions out loud and answer. If time permits, allow other children to contribute their ideas. After they have shared their answers for each question, share with them how Saran would answer the questions.

CONSERVATION TIP: THE AVERAGE AMERICAN BATH USES 37 GALLONS OF WATER, AND A SHORT SHOWER USES 20 GALLONS.

1. How do you get your water at your house? (In Bangladesh, Saran pumps the water from a tube well in the ground.)

2. What chores do you have at your house? (Saran helps plant the seeds for crops, gives water to the calves on the farm, and looks after pigeons.)

3. How many baths do you take a day? (Saran takes three baths a day because it is so hot in Bangladesh.)

4. How much water do you use to take a bath? (Saran uses four mugs of water for a morning bath and one mug each for afternoon and evening baths.)

5. How do you wash your clothes? (Saran's family washes their clothes first in a pond, then in water from the wells.)

6. What fun thing do you like to do with water? (Saran's favorite thing is swimming.)

7. Do you do anything special before you come to church? (Saran is Muslim and goes to a mosque instead of a church. Before entering the building to pray, he cleans his face, hands, and feet.)

Say, "In Bangladesh, people have to worry about flooding because it rains so much. Homes can get washed away. Did you do an activity today that would help people stay safe from floods?" (Let the children share the homes they designed and talk about the levees they built.)

CLOSING

Reviewing

Use this time to talk about the other activities and tie all the day's activities and study together. Use the following prompts:

- What new thing did you learn about water today?
- What was your favorite activity today? Why?
- When you see a rainbow in the sky, what does it make you think of?

PARTING PRAYER

We give thanks, O God, for the rainbow in the sky following the rain. May the rainbow always remind us of your love for all creation and that the gift of water is a good gift to be respected and enjoyed with care. Amen.

THREE

Moses in the Basket on the Nile River

SCRIPTURE TEXT
Exodus 1:8–10, 22; 2:1–10

FOCUS OF THE DAY
Water is God's sacred gift to the world.

PURPOSE OF THE LESSON
*To explore different ways that water manifests itself
on the earth, as well as a variety of ways that water can become
sacred for different peoples of the world*

FOR THE LEADER—AN OPENING MEDITATION

The story of Moses being placed in the basket and floated down the river at first glance appears to be a warm and fuzzy story. Many of us learned it as children in a Sunday school kindergarten class. However, the background of the story is tragic and violent. Baby Moses was placed in a basket and floated down the river as a desperate attempt of a distraught mother to try to save his life! As the story goes, all the Hebrew boys were being killed by the king of Egypt because the Hebrew people were growing in numbers so fast the Egyptians were becoming afraid that the Hebrew population would grow to the point of leading an uprising and revolt. How do we handle such a violent story with our children?

At first we may want to shy away from this story, thinking it is more than our children can bear. But before we are too hasty, let us recall that many of the classic children's stories are based on violent themes—"Little Red Riding Hood" and "Hansel and Gretel," just to name two. Bruno Bettleheim, in his classic work *The Uses of Enchantment: The Meaning and Importance of Fairy Tales,* contends it is important for children to be able to deal with such stories, as it enables them to grow, mature, and learn how to deal with the challenges and tragedies of our world. So while we may not want to dwell on the point that Pharaoh commanded that all the Hebrew boys be killed at birth or thrown into the Nile River, perhaps we do our children a disservice if we ignore it. Such is a matter that each leader will need to navigate depending on the setting, the age and maturity of the children participating, and so on.

The good news is that every baby is important, and every baby deserves a chance to grow up and make a positive difference in the world. In this particular story, and in keeping with the theme of this study, water was the salvation—it became sacred—for the baby Moses. In many ways water becomes sacred in diverse ways and for various peoples of the world. For the Jewish people, the water of the Red Sea, the water from the rock in the wilderness, and water in other instances was significant. For Christians, water baptism holds sacred significance, and for Muslims washing the face is a sacred, religious ritual. For the Hindus ritual washing in the Ganges River is a major event.

Let us be reminded, as we relive the story of the baby Moses' being saved in the water of the Nile, just how important and sacred water has been throughout history.

GATHERING TIME

Welcome the children back. Ask what they remember about the last lesson. (Possible responses include the water cycle, Noah, small group activities, and Bangladesh.)

Say, "Today we're going to learn some cool stuff about frozen water. What do we call frozen water? (ice) Then we'll hear a Bible story about a baby who took a ride on a river, do some fun activities, and learn what it's like to live in a country called Peru.

"But first, let's sing our water song, 'Itsy Bitsy Raindrops.'" (Or use the alternate hymn.)

Gathering Music

"Itsy, Bitsy Raindrops" (Words by Dot Keller; tune: "Itsy, Bitsy Spider")

Itsy, bitsy raindrops are falling all around.
On the streets and sidewalks and on the sun-baked ground.
Making green our flowers and quenching thirsty trees.
Itsy, bitsy raindrops are falling down on me.

Or sing "To You, O God, All Creatures Sing" (*The New Century Hymnal* #17, verse 3).

WHOLE GROUP ACTIVITY
Why It Is Important That Ice Floats

Purpose

To demonstrate to children that solid water floats in liquid water and to help them understand why this is important

Materials

- empty two-liter bottle with lid
- empty water bottle with lid, any size
- ice cube
- bin large enough to hold the two-liter bottle
- tarp or newspapers
- safety goggles
- knife
- cooler
- kitchen towels or newspapers

Preparation

Fill the bottles almost full with water, screw on the lids, and freeze at least overnight.

Shortly before the demonstration, you'll need to get the ice out of the bottles. Put on the safety goggles and use the knife to cut the bottle away from the ice. Be careful, as sometimes the ice expands and pops. If the ice breaks into pieces, don't worry; use the biggest pieces. Put the ice from the bottles and the ice cube in a cooler and cover with either a towel or newspapers. This is to keep the contents a surprise.

Spread the tarp or newspapers on the floor and put the bin on it.

Put water in the bin, leaving enough room for the water to rise when you add the ice.

Procedure

Gather the children around the bin and ask, "Has anyone ever been swimming in a lake? Maybe you've noticed that the deeper you go in a lake, the colder the water gets. That's because cold water is heavier than warm water, so it sinks. What do you think happens when water gets so cold that it freezes?" (Let kids give their ideas, but don't tell them the answer.)

Say, "Let's find out." Take the small ice cube out of the cooler and show the kids. "I have an ice cube here. Let's put it in the water and see what happens." Toss the cube in.

"Did the cube sink?" Let the children answer. "Well, that was a pretty small piece of ice. Let's try a bigger piece." Take the next size piece of ice out and set it in the water. "Did that ice sink?"

Finally, take out the biggest piece of ice. "Okay, this is a really big piece of ice. Let's see what happens now." Set the ice in the water. You can push it down and let it bob back up. "So what do you think? Does ice sink? No, it doesn't. Cold liquid water does sink, but water that's so cold that it turns to ice floats on top."

"Can anyone think why it is important that ice floats? Think what would happen to a lake if ice sank to the bottom." Give the children a chance to share their ideas. You can guide them with these questions:

- If the ice sank to the bottom, then the water on top of the lake would get really cold and freeze. Then what would happen to it? (It would sink to the bottom, too.)
- After awhile, the whole lake would be frozen. Then what would happen to the animals and plants in the lake? (They would die.)

Point out that, as the children saw, ice doesn't sink, it floats. So since the ice is sitting on top of the water, it keeps the cold air away from the rest of the water in the lake. So that water doesn't freeze. And the plants and animals can live though the winter.

STUDYING

Focus of the Day

Water is God's sacred gift to the world.

Bible Story: Exodus 1:8–10, 22; 2:1–10 (paraphrased)

A long, long time ago, there was a man named Jacob. Jacob had a large family. In the land where Jacob and his family lived, there came a drought. Can anyone tell us what a drought is? It didn't rain for a long time, so the ground became very dry. This led to a famine. What is a famine? A famine is when no food can grow on the earth because there is no rain and the earth becomes too dry.

Well, since there was no drought or famine in Egypt, that is where Jacob moved his family, because there was food in Egypt. When Jacob moved his family to Egypt, everyone there liked them, including the king of Egypt, who knew Jacob's family well.

However, over time the king who knew Jacob died, and Jacob and all of his children died. But Jacob's family grew tremendously. They were now called the Hebrews. A new king came to the throne in Egypt, who did not know or care about Jacob's family, the Hebrews.

The new king said to the leaders in his court, "There are getting to be so many of these Hebrews, and they are growing so strong. What if they decided to turn against us? We must find some way to keep their numbers from growing so fast." So the king issued a command that when the Hebrew mothers gave birth to a baby boy, the women who helped deliver the baby should kill it. But these women knew that was the wrong thing to do, so they refused to do it. Since that didn't work, the king said, "Every newborn Hebrew boy shall be thrown into the Nile River."

Well, at this time a Hebrew man and woman had a baby boy. He was a fine-looking baby boy. Knowing what the king had ordered, the mother and father hid their baby boy for three months. But when the baby's cry got so loud that they could not hide him anymore, the mother tried to think of a way to save his life, to keep him from being thrown into the Nile River. So here is what she did. She took a basket made out of river reeds, and she covered it with tar so it would not leak. She carefully wrapped the baby boy in a blanket and placed him in the basket and then let the basket float at the edge of the river. She thought, *Maybe someone will find him, feel sorry for him, and save him.* The baby's big sister hid in the tall grass to watch and see who might find her baby brother.

It just so happened that the king's daughter, the Egyptian princess, came down to the river for a swim. Suddenly, the king's daughter saw the basket floating in the water, and she sent one of her servants to get it. When the princess opened the basket she was surprised to find a baby boy. The baby was crying, which made the princess very sad. She could tell that he was one of the Hebrew babies.

The baby's big sister, who was watching in the tall grass far away, ran over and said, "Would you like me to get one of the Hebrew women to care for the baby for you?"

"Oh yes," the princess said. So the baby's sister ran home and brought her mother to meet the princess. The princess said, "Take this baby home and protect him and care for him, and I will pay you." So that is what the mother did—she took the baby home, her own baby boy, and she cared for him.

When the boy was old enough, she took him to the princess, who adopted him as her own son. The Hebrew boy grew up in the palace with the princess. And the princess said, "Since I pulled him out of the water, I am going to call him Moses, because the name Moses sounds like the Hebrew word that means 'pull out of the water.'"

Well, the years passed and Moses became a man and a great leader. And he was the one who would lead his people out of slavery into a new land. He was also the one who would give his people and the whole world the Ten Commandments.

And that is the story of the baby Moses and how the Nile River floated his basket to the princess and enabled him to be saved.

Question and Discussion Time

1. Why did the king of Egypt command that all the Hebrew baby boys be destroyed? (They feared the Hebrews would become so numerous they would rebel and cause trouble.)

2. What did Moses' mother do to try to save his life? (She put him in a basket and floated him down the river.)

3. Who found baby Moses in the basket? (The king's daughter found him.)

4. Whom did the king's daughter pay to take care of baby Moses until he got older? (She paid his own mother.)

5. What did Moses grow up to become? (He became a great leader, the one who led his people out of slavery to freedom.)

EXPLORING — SMALL GROUP ACTIVITIES

Note: Do Activity One before you break into small groups. The experiment can be set up and then checked on at the beginning of the Regrouping time.

ACTIVITY ONE: Ice Cube Challenge

Purpose

To experiment with ways to keep an ice cube from melting

Materials

- ice cubes (one or two per child)
- newspapers
- plastic wrap
- foil
- cloth scraps/old socks
- string
- tape
- styrofoam pieces
- zip style baggies
- paper towels or towels (to clean up spills)
- plastic grocery bags (for collecting experiments later)

Procedure

Tell the children that for this activity they are going to experiment with ways to keep an ice cube from melting. Show the children the various materials and tell them to select one or two to wrap around an ice cube. They can secure their materials with string, tape, or a baggie. Then hand each child one or two ice cubes.

Once they have insulated their ice cubes, let them choose where to place them. If they have two ice cubes, they can experiment with two ideas. Leave the ice cubes until the end of the Small Group Activities.

ACTIVITY TWO: Diorama of Moses on the Nile River

Purpose

To let the children build a visual representation of the Moses in the basket story

Materials

(Children can be creative with almost any materials, so start with what you have on hand and purchase extras if necessary. The following list includes suggestions.)

- homemade play dough (See recipe, p. 29, "Preparation")
- toilet paper tubes
- construction paper
- craft foam
- craft sticks
- fabric scraps
- tape
- markers
- pipe cleaners/chenille sticks
- blue paper, tissue paper, wrapping paper, or cloth
- picture book that shows ancient Egyptian clothing

Preparation

Prepare a river by cutting a long piece (or taping together pieces) of paper, tissue paper, wrapping paper, or cloth. The children will make things to go on and around the river.

Procedure

Remind the children of the story they heard about Moses. Show them the blue paper and say this represents the river in the story. Ask them to think of some things that should go on or around the river. If they need help, you can suggest a baby in a basket, animals, such as crocodiles, plants to go on the edges, the princess who found the baby, and Moses' sister Miriam.

Show the children the supplies and tell them to choose something to make to go in the scene. They can make as many things as they like. Don't worry if all the children want to make the same thing or make something purely imaginative. If you like, you can make some other things to go along, as well.

ACTIVITY THREE: Paper Weaving (especially for younger children)

Purpose

To mimic weaving, as in the story of Moses, by making a two-dimensional craft

Materials

- black construction paper (9 x 12 inches), one per child
- various colors of construction paper (9 x 12 inches)
- scissors
- paper cutter, if available
- cellophane tape
- glue
- glitter (optional)
- markers (optional)

FUN FACT: THE LONGEST RIVER IN THE WORLD IS THE NILE RIVER. IT IS 6650 KILOMETERS (4132 MILES) IN LENGTH.

Preparation

Fold the black paper in half crosswise and, beginning at the fold, cut slits that go to within an inch or two of the other side.

Using the paper cutter, if available, cut the colored paper into crosswise strips, one to two inches wide. They can be the same width or vary in width.

Procedure

Give each child a sheet of prepared black paper. Make accessible the colorful strips.

Tell them to choose a strip and show them how to weave it by going under and over the slits. When they get to the end, they should push the strip to the top of the paper.

Take a second strip and weave it, but in the reverse of the first. If the first began under a slit, the second should begin over the slit. Continue weaving strips until the paper is full.

Glue or tape the ends to the black paper.

(Optional) Children can decorate the weaving with glitter and markers, if they like.

ACTIVITY FOUR: Paper Basket Weaving (especially for older children)

Purpose

To mimic the woven basket in the story of the baby Moses

Materials

- card stock, various colors
- paper cutter, if available
- scissors
- child-safe scissors
- cellophane tape
- ruler

Preparation

Cut the card stock lengthwise into one-inch wide strips. Each basket will need thirteen strips.

Procedure

Remind the children that Moses' mother wove a basket for him. Tell them they are going to weave their own baskets from paper.

Let each child choose eight strips of paper. Guide them to lay four strips horizontally and close together on the table. Tape one end of each strip to the table to hold it in place.

Weave the other four strips into the horizontal strips. Show the children how to alternate over and under. If they begin one strip by going over the first horizontal strip and under the next, then they should begin the next strip by going under the first horizontal strip and over the next. After they have woven all the strips together, they should push them as close together as possible to make a tightly woven square. The square should be as centered as possible.

Now you have a square of woven paper, with the excess out to each of the four sides. Fold up the excess to get a basket shape. Use four more strips and weave them in and out of these vertical strips. You may need to tape the strips to keep them from moving. As children get to the end of one strip, have them tape it down and begin with another strip.

Instruct them to keep weaving until they have three horizontal rows. Then tape all the loose ends down.

Use the final strip to make a handle. Tape one end on the inside of the basket and the other end on the opposite side.

ACTIVITY FIVE: How Does a Glacier Move?

Purpose

To demonstrate the different ways a glacier can move

Note: Oobleck is loads of fun. This is a good activity for children who need tactile experiences.

CAUTION: Do not dispose of oobleck down the drain; it can clog the pipes.

Materials

- cornstarch
- water
- large mixing pan, such as a cake pan
- large spoon

- measuring cup or spoons
- disposable bowls
- small spoons
- bucket
- tarp or newspapers
- picture of glacier

Preparation

If you've never made oobleck before, try making some ahead of time to get a feel for it. As you combine the cornstarch and water, you'll reach a point when you cannot stir it anymore; you'll have to use your hands to mix it completely. Play with it to get an idea of the difference it makes to apply pressure quickly or slowly, for example, hitting it with a fist versus letting your finger sink into it, or holding some in your hand, letting it ooze through your fingers, then quickly clenching your fist around it. You may want to make the oobleck ahead of time for the children, but it's also interesting to them to watch it being prepared or to prepare it themselves.

If you are working indoors, spread a tarp or newspapers on the floor to contain the mess.

Put water in the bucket for cleaning hands at the end of the activity.

Procedure

Before you begin the activity, show the children the picture of a glacier and tell them that in some parts of the world it stays so cold all year that the ice doesn't melt. Instead, it piles up year after year, until it is really thick, even as thick as thousands of feet. We call big fields of thick ice glaciers. Glaciers don't stand still, even though it looks like they do. They move very slowly, sometimes a few feet a day, but sometimes only an inch a day. Glaciers can be brittle and crack or they can be bendy, sort of like plastic. Tell the children that in this activity they are going to play with something else that can break or bend, depending on how they handle it.

Decide if you want to mix the oobleck before giving some to each child or allow each child to mix his or her own.

Give each child a disposable bowl and a small spoon. If children are mixing their own, put 5 tablespoons of cornstarch in each bowl, then add 2 tablespoons of water. Let them mix it together, using their fingers when it gets difficult to stir.

If you are mixing it, use the same proportions of 5 to 2 and add cornstarch to the cake pan, then the water, mixing with the large spoon, using your hands when it gets difficult. Once it is mixed, give it to the children in their bowls.

Let the children play with the oobleck as long as they like, or as time allows. While they are doing so, suggest they try things like poking it, letting their fingers rest on top of it (they'll sink), holding it in their hands and letting it ooze through their fingers, then grasping it quickly. Help them notice how the oobleck behaves differently, according to how fast and hard they handle it. Glaciers are similar—they can flow or they can break.

When children are finished, have them dispose of their bowls in the garbage. Do not put the oobleck down the drain. Instruct the children to rinse their hands off in the bucket of water before washing them in a sink. (Pour the water outside when you are done.)

ACTIVITY SIX: Waterproofing Newspaper Bowls

Purpose

To experiment with different ways of waterproofing a newspaper bowl

Materials

- plastic bowls (cereal bowls are a good size)
- lots of newspaper
- masking tape
- vegetable shortening
- oil
- butter
- petroleum jelly
- sunscreen
- large bin
- water

CONSERVATION TIP: A LEAKY TOILET CAN WASTE 600 GALLONS OF WATER EACH MONTH.

Preparation

Cut newspapers to fit over the outside of the bowl.

Fill the bin with water.

Procedure

Remind the children that in the story of Moses, his mother waterproofed his basket with tar so that it would float on the Nile River.

Give each child three to four pieces of newspaper stacked together.

Turn a bowl upside down and instruct the child to cover the bowl with newspaper and shape it to the bowl, tucking the edges inside the bowl.

Let the child tape around the outside of the bowl, near the rim. Remove the bowl from the newspaper. If the newspaper does not hold the bowl shape, use more masking tape. Let the child make two newspaper bowls.

Let the child float one newspaper bowl in the water, and observe that it sinks.

Show the child the various waterproofing agents and allow her or him to smear one on the outside of the second bowl and set it in the water. Does it float? If the child would like, she or he can make multiple bowls to test the different waterproofing agents. Discuss with the child which agent worked best.

ACTIVITY SEVEN: God's Eyes

Purpose

To learn that, in Peru, some people raise an animal called an alpaca for its fur and to make an ornament with yarn to remind them of this

Materials

- craft sticks
- hot glue gun

- hot glue sticks
- yarn of various colors
- scissors
- picture of an alpaca (optional)

Preparation

Use the hot glue gun to glue two craft sticks together to make a cross. Make as many crosses as you need.

Procedure

If you have a photo of an alpaca, show it to the children while you tell them that alpacas are animals raised for their fur by people in a country called Peru. The fur is turned into yarn to make clothing and blankets.

Give each child a cross and let them select a yarn. They can add different colors as they go along or use only one color.

Help children tie the yarn at the center of the cross.

Wrap the yarn around one of the sticks, then around the next stick, all the way around. Continue until the cross is about two-thirds full, changing colors along the way if desired. Knot the yarn around one of the sticks to finish.

ACTIVITY EIGHT: Make an Alpaca (for younger children)

Purpose

To make an alpaca and learn that these animals are raised in Peru for their fur

Materials

- card stock
- yarn (cream and light brown for authenticity, but any color will do)
- scissors
- tape
- glue
- picture of an alpaca

Preparation

Cut card stock in half crosswise, then fold each half in half, also crosswise.

Cutting from the end opposite the fold and leaving one inch on each side, cut out a rectangle that measures two inches from the bottom. What's left should look roughly like a body with legs. Now, beginning at the edge, cut a slit about one to one and a half inches along the fold.

Next from card stock, cut a shape that looks roughly like the neck and head of an alpaca. The neck should be long and the head small.

Procedure

Tell the children that in Peru some people raise an animal called an alpaca for its fur. The fur can be turned into yarn that can be woven into blankets and clothing. In this activity, they'll make their own alpaca.

Give each child a body and a neck. Show them how to insert the neck into the slit at the top of the body and tape it. They now have an alpaca, but it needs fur.

Let the child choose a yarn. Help them tape the end to the body and let them wrap the yarn around the body. Show them how to wrap loosely so that the body can be spread apart for the alpaca to stand.

Optional: Younger children can cut pieces of yarn and glue them to the body.

ACTIVITY NINE: Nazca Lines

Purpose

To introduce children to an interesting feature of Peru

Materials

- scrap pieces of cardboard or cereal boxes
- sand
- three-ounce disposable cups
- liquid glue (not glue sticks)
- pencils
- newspapers

Preparation

Do an Internet search for Nazca Lines and print out pictures to show the children. (Check out these links for photos: *http://ngm.nationalgeographic.com/2010/03/nasca/clark-photography* or *http://www.go2peru.com/gal_nazca01.htm.*)

Make simple line drawings similar to the Nazca lines.

Procedure

Tell the children that people who lived a long time ago in the country of Peru etched huge drawings in the desert sand that we can still see today. These drawings are so big that you can see them from an airplane. Show the children the photos of the drawings and tell them that they can make a small model of these drawings.

Cover the work area with newspaper and give each child a piece of cardboard, a pencil, and a cup of sand. Show them the simple drawings you made. Tell them they can draw something similar to what they see in the photos or to your drawings or they can design their own simple drawing.

Once they have drawn lines on their cardboard, they can go over the lines with the glue.

Finally, they can shake sand over the lines, tapping the excess onto the newspaper.

ACTIVITY TEN: Experimenting with Temperature and Density in Water

Purpose

To help children grasp the concept that cold water is heavier than warm water, but that frozen water is lighter

Note: You can set this activity up as a demonstration or for individual explorations. If you do a larger group demonstration, use a large clear container for the warm water and a pitcher for the cold water. If you are doing individual explorations, use clear plastic cups and straws.

Materials

- large, clear plastic container or clear plastic cups
- straws
- very warm water
- ice cold water (but not frozen)
- blue food coloring
- cooler
- ice cubes
- one or two pitchers or three ounce cups

Preparation

You will need a pitcher with ice cold water, a container of ice cubes, and a pitcher or container of warm water.

Add food dye to the ice cold water and set it and the container of ice cubes in the cooler. You can use any color of dye, but since we associate blue with cold, it might help the children remember that the cold water is sinking.

Procedure

Help the children recall what they learned in the Whole Group time about water as it gets colder. (As water gets colder, it sinks because it gets heavier. But when it gets so cold that it turns to ice, it gets lighter than the liquid water and floats.)

Tell them that this activity will let them see water sinking and ice floating.

If you are letting children explore on their own, give each a plastic cup of warm water and a straw. Show them how to dip the straw into the cold water and then cover the top of the straw with their finger to keep the water from running out.

This works better if the water in the cup is still, so let the cup sit undisturbed for a few moments. Tell the children to hold the straw just below the surface of the warm water and let go of their fingers. The cold water will sink to the bottom of the cup. Ask the children why this happened. (The cold water is heavier.)

You can also reverse the warm and cold, giving the children cups of icy cold water and warm water with food dye. Follow the same procedure, only this time the water will stay nearer the surface.

Next give each child an ice cube to put in his or her cup of water. Ask them what happens. (The ice floats.) Why? (Ice is lighter than liquid water.)

Optional: Let the children explore. Ask them if an ice cube behaves differently in warm water than in cold water. Give each child a cup of warm water and a cup of cold water and let them see.

ACTIVITY ELEVEN: Wash Day Relay

Purpose

To wash clothes in a tub and hang them to dry

Materials

- large tub or two buckets
- clothing, such as t-shirts

- rope or clothes line
- clothes pins
- biodegradable soap
- hose
- access to water

Preparation

Find a suitable place for the relay: a soft surface, such as grass, with two objects to tie the rope between to make a clothesline at child's height.

The clothesline marks one end of the relay course. Put the large tub or two buckets by the clothesline, easily accessible to the children.

Fill the tub with soapy water and add the clothes.

Pin clothespins to the line or have an adult ready to hand them to the children.

Procedure

Divide children into two groups and line them up at the end of the course opposite the clothesline.

Tell them that in some parts of the world, people don't have washing machines and have to wash their clothes by hand and hang them up to dry.

Instruct the children to run to the other end of the course, pick out a piece of clothing, wring it out, and hang it on the clothesline, using the clothespins.

Then they should run back so the next child in line can take a turn.

Helpful Hints: Clothespins can be difficult for younger children, so you may want to let them just lay the clothes across the line.

If you don't have as many clothes as you have children, let a couple of adults stand behind the clothesline and throw clothes back in the washtub.

REGROUPING — STORY TIME

Note: Before children come back for the regrouping time, have them collect their ice cubes. Tell them not to open them, yet. You may need to provide plastic grocery bags for drippy experiments.

Book: *The Story of Snow: The Science of Winter's Wonder* by Mark Cassino with Jon Nelson, Ph.D. (San Francisco: Chronicle Books, 2009). *Note:* You don't need to read every word in this book; the photos of snowflakes will probably most interest the children.

WHOLE GROUP ACTIVITIES

ACTIVITY ONE: Discussing the Country of the Day—Peru

Purpose

To locate Peru on the map and discover its annual rainfall

Materials

- map of continents
- two labels marked Peru
- tape
- blue yarn, two inches long

Preparation

Make sure you know where Peru is located.

Procedure

Say, "Today we are going to learn about a boy named Lucas who lives in Peru.

"Does anyone know what continent Peru is on?" (South America) "Where is South America?" (Use the map you hung on the wall the first day.) "Very good. Now does anyone know about where Peru is?" Show the children the approximate location of Peru on the map and let a child attach the label with tape.

"This week, we've been looking at how much rain falls in a year in different places around the world. Who can tell me how much rain we get in our town? What about in Bangladesh? Now, who would like to guess how much rain falls in a year in Peru?" Give children a chance to answer, then tell them that it depends on where you are in Peru. Peru is on the ocean, but it also has jungles and deserts. The jungle gets about 150 inches of rain every year. But most people don't live in the jungle; most live on the coast. The coast gets less than two inches of rain every year. Show the children the two-inch yarn. Ask, "That's not very much rain, is it?" Tape the yarn to the wall, with a Peru label.

ACTIVITY TWO: Comparing Our Lives

Purpose

To compare the children's daily lives with that of a boy who lives in Peru

Materials

- book, *Our World of Water* by Beatrice Hollyer
- bucket(s) of ice cold water
- paper towels

Procedure

Say, "Let's look at our child of the day." (Show photos from the book *Our World of Water.*) "His name is Lucas and he lives high in the mountains in Peru. His family has a herd of eight hundred alpacas. Did anyone learn about alpacas today?" (Yes, from the God's-eye activity and the alpaca activity) "Alpaca fur is woven into yarn and people make clothing and blankets from it."

Tell the children that, where Lucas lives, much of the water people use comes from glaciers. Some people don't have heated water, so the water coming out of their faucets is ice cold. Can they imagine what it would be like to wash their hands and faces in ice cold water first thing in the morning? Well that's exactly what Lucas has to do. Every morning, he gets up and washes his hands and face in water that comes from glaciers. Because they don't have heated water in their house, the water is ice cold.

Show the kids the bucket(s) of ice cold water. Encourage them to dip their hands in it and even put some on their faces. This is what Lucas has to do every morning.

Finally, have the children open their ice-cube experiments and compare results. Provide paper towels or towels to clean up spills. Which insulation did the best job? Did it make a difference where the child stored his or her ice cube?

Tell the children that we like to keep our ice frozen because we use it to cool our drinks, or to put in coolers for picnics. But if the ice does melt, it isn't really a big deal. However, sometimes melting ice is a big deal. Lucas lives on a mountain. Where does his water come from? (A glacier) A glacier is a huge sheet of ice and the glacier near Lucas's town is melting. The mountain near his hometown used to be white with snow and ice, but now it is almost bare.

Scientists are learning what causes these big glaciers to melt. It is important for all of us to remember that our lives are intertwined and to learn ways we can help protect these huge mountains of ice and the people who depend on them.

CLOSING

Reviewing

Invite discussion with these questions:

- Did you learn anything new about water today that you didn't already know?
- What was the most interesting thing you discovered about water, snow, or ice?
- Share something interesting you learned about Peru.

PARTING PRAYER

Remembering the prayer of Francis of Assisi, we give thanks to you, O God, for Sister Water, who is very useful and humble and precious and pure. Amen.

FOUR

The Baptism of Jesus in the Jordan River

SCRIPTURE TEXT
Matthew 3:13–17

VERSE OF THE DAY
As Jesus was baptized, . . . he saw the Spirit of God coming down
like a dove and lighting on him. (Matthew 3:16 GNT)

PURPOSE OF THE LESSON
To consider different ways that different people around the world
consider water to be sacred, as well as the great effort that some people
of the world go to in order to acquire life-giving water

FOR THE LEADER—AN OPENING MEDITATION

Water has been used sacramentally for millennia. That is, water has been set apart from a common to a sacred use for the purpose of religious observances—to mark new beginnings, to symbolize spiritual cleansing, to initiate a person into a group and new way of living.

At first, one might think that Jesus, who traditionally has been thought of as being sin-free, had no need for baptism, since baptism for John the Baptist was a ritual indicating a washing away of sin. But baptism is rich and diverse in meaning and symbolism.

As a devout, religious man, it was only natural that Jesus would receive a rite involving water since such rites are so universal in orientation. Many world religions have employed rituals involving water, including Hinduism, Judaism, Christianity, and Islam.

We do well to remember, however, that water need not be prayed over or blessed, as in baptism, to be sacred. As one of God's greatest gifts, all water on earth is sacred. Every time we take a drink, or draw a soothing bath, or wash dirt or germs from our hands, or use water to cook our vegetables, we do well to take a moment to breathe a prayer of thanks for this most wonderful gift—water. Sacred water.

GATHERING TIME

Welcome the children back. Ask what they remember about the last session. (Possible responses include ice, Moses, small group activities, and Peru.)

Say, "Today, we're going to learn what water is made of, hear a Bible story about Jesus, do some fun activities, and learn what it's like to live in a country called Tajikistan.

"Let's start with our water song." (Or use the alternate hymn.)

Gathering Music

"Itsy, Bitsy Raindrops" (Words by Dot Keller; tune: "Itsy, Bitsy Spider")

Itsy-bitsy raindrops are falling all around.
On the streets and sidewalks and on the sun-baked ground.
Making green our flowers and quenching thirsty trees.
Itsy, bitsy raindrops are falling down on me.

Or sing "Come, O Fount of Every Blessing" (*The New Century Hymnal* #459, verse 1).

WHOLE GROUP ACTIVITY
What Is a Water Molecule?

Purpose

To help children begin to understand that a molecule is the smallest amount you can have of water (and most things) and that if you break a molecule into parts, those parts are different from the molecule and are called atoms.

Materials

- two-liter bottle with cap
- one-liter bottle with cap
- measuring cups
- measuring spoons
- medicine dropper
- water
- bowl
- funnel
- small piece of wax paper
- toothpick
- sheet of paper
- marker

Preparation

Fill the two-liter bottle with water. Write "H_2O" on the paper.

Procedure

Show the children the two-liter bottle and ask them what is in it. (water)

Let a child hold the one-liter bottle while you use the funnel to fill it with water from the two-liter bottle. Screw the cap on the two-liter and set it aside. Now ask the children what is in the one-liter bottle. (water) To keep their interest throughout, you'll have to continue to show interest in the water, asking as though you aren't sure what's in the bottle.

Continue this process, pouring the water from larger to smaller measuring cups, asking the children what is in the new measuring cup each time. Occasionally, you can ask, "So it's still water even though it's not as much?" Remember that children like to show how much they know, so you can question them, "Are you sure it's still water?"

When you've poured water into the smallest container, use the measuring spoons to scoop out smaller amounts, finally ending with the medicine dropper.

Using the medicine dropper, place a drop on the wax paper and ask the children again if it's still water.

Use the toothpick to break the water drop into droplets. When you get the drop about as small as you can, ask the children if what you have is still water.

Agree with the children that no matter how small you made the water, it was still water. Tell them that if you continue to divide the water into smaller pieces, you would get to the very smallest piece you can. It would be so small that you would only be able to see it with a special microscope that only scientists have. This smallest piece has a name—water molecule. If you divide a water molecule up, you won't have water anymore, you'll have smaller pieces called atoms. In nature, atoms stick together to make up different things. Water molecules are made of three atoms. Two of those atoms are called hydrogen and one is called oxygen.

Ask the children if they have ever heard of H_2O. Most likely some of them have. Show them the index card and tell them this is how that is written. Do they know what it means? It means water: two hydrogen atoms and one oxygen atom—that's what water is made of.

STUDYING

Verse of the Day

"As Jesus was baptized, . . . he saw the Spirit of God coming down like a dove and lighting on him." (Matthew 3:16 GNT)

Bible Story: Matthew 3:13–17 (paraphrased)

A long time ago, there was a man named John who was called John the Baptizer because he baptized people in the Jordan River who came out into the wilderness to hear him preach. In those days pouring water on people's heads, or dipping people in water, was a popular religious practice that symbolized the washing away of the wrong things people had done.

One day Jesus came out into the wilderness and asked to be baptized by John. And John said, "I don't understand. You don't need to be baptized. I should be baptized by you." But Jesus insisted, saying it needed to be done since it would be pleasing to God. So John agreed and baptized Jesus. When Jesus was baptized, God's Spirit came down and lighted on him, like a dove might do. And a voice from heaven said, "This is my son, whom I love very much."

Question and Discussion Time

1. Have you seen someone—a baby or a child or even an adult—be baptized?

2. What substance was used in the baptism?

3. How was the water used?

4. Why do you think water is used in baptism?

5. Do you think the water used in baptism is given a meaning in addition to its common one?

EXPLORING—SMALL GROUP ACTIVITIES

ACTIVITY ONE: Making a Dove (especially for younger children)

Purpose

To help children recall the Bible story by making a fun craft

Materials

- miniature marshmallows
- glue
- wax paper or scrap paper
- card stock or construction paper
- picture of a dove
- crayons

Procedure

Help the children recall the Bible story. How was the spirit of God described? (It was like a dove.)

Tell the children that to help them remember the story, they are going to make a picture of a dove with marshmallows.

Give each child a piece of card stock or construction paper and a crayon. Show them the picture of the dove and ask them to draw an outline of a dove on their paper. Assure them that their dove doesn't have to look like the picture, that the picture is just to give them an idea of what a dove looks like.

Once they have their outline completed, give them a piece of wax paper or scrap paper and pour some glue on it. Then give them a handful of marshmallows.

Show the children how to dip the end of the marshmallow in the glue, then glue the marshmallow onto the paper. Replenish the marshmallows as needed. Very young children may just want to glue the marshmallows onto the paper, which is fine.

ACTIVITY TWO: Make a Water Wheel

Purpose

To help children understand how water can be used for work

Note: The water wheel in this activity won't last for long, but it will give children an idea of how water wheels turn.

Materials

- disposable foam bowls
- egg cartons
- glue sticks
- masking tape or duct tape
- thin dowel rods
- pencil
- picture of water wheel
- cups
- water
- bucket or sink (if indoors)

Preparation

Cut the egg cartons into individual cups. Foam cartons are better, but cardboard will work for a short time.

Cut dowel rods to about 12 inches. Make sure there are no splinters.

Procedure

Remind the children of the Bible story. Ask them where Jesus was baptized (in the Jordan River). Tell the children that rivers have always been important to people. One way that rivers are important is that we can put them to work. If you have a picture of a water wheel, show the children and say, "Long ago, people used rivers to turn water wheels. When the wheels turned, they could be used, for example, to grind corn or wheat."

Give each child two bowls, five to six egg carton cups, access to glue sticks, and tape.

To make the wheel, first cover the bottom of one bowl with glue, then attach it to the bottom of the second bowl. The glue should bond pretty quickly.

Next, use tape to attach the egg cups to the seam where the two bowls are joined. Make sure that the cups are all facing the same direction as you turn the bowls.

Next, poke a hole in the center of the bottoms of the bowls, using the pencil. The hole needs to be bigger than the dowel rod, so the wheel will turn easily. Slide the dowel rod through the hole.

Finally, while someone holds the dowel rod, let the child pour water so that it fills the egg cups. The wheel should turn.

ACTIVITY THREE: Water Harvesting

Purpose

To introduce children to the idea of water harvesting while enjoying a fun activity

Materials

- half-inch PVC pipes
- PVC connectors, such as elbows, crosses, tees, and couplings
- saw (for adult use only)
- goggles
- file or coarse sandpaper
- funnels
- shallow containers
- plastic pitcher
- water

Preparation

Use the saw (hand or electric) to cut the PVC pipes into various lengths. Be careful when using an electric saw, as the PVC pipes can splinter. Be sure to wear goggles and preferably a face shield, if possible. Sawing slowly may help reduce splintering.

Use the file or coarse sandpaper to smooth any rough edges.

Procedure

Tell children that some places in the world don't get much rain. People who live there try to collect as much rain as they can instead of just letting it run on the ground. When they collect it, they can use the water where it is most needed, such as watering crops. This is called water harvesting. One way to harvest water is to catch the rain that runs off of roofs. We see an example of this in our own country when people collect rain from their gutters into a rain barrel.

Tell the children that in this activity, they are going to collect water in a funnel and use pipes to make the water go where they want it to go.

Show them the PVC pipes and various connectors, and demonstrate how to put them together. Let them play with putting the pipes and connectors together in various configurations.

When they are ready to try their configuration out, they should insert the funnel into one pipe and pour water in it. If their configuration is flat, they will need to tilt it up. Or they can use an elbow joint to make one of the pipes vertical.

Talk with the children about what is happening. If they have several openings, is the water flowing more quickly out some than others? If they reduce the number of openings, will the water come out more quickly?

If you want to reuse the water, place shallow containers at the end of the pipes for the water to flow into.

ACTIVITY FOUR: Make a Water Molecule

Purpose

To remind children that the smallest piece of water is called a water molecule and that the molecule is made of two hydrogen atoms and one oxygen atom

Materials

- modeling compound, such as modeling clay (at least two colors)
- small paper plates

Procedure

Ask the children what they remember about water molecules. Help them recall that the smallest piece of water is called a water molecule and that if you break the molecule into smaller pieces, you get atoms, two hydrogen atoms and one oxygen atom.

Tell the children that they will make a model of a water molecule. Remind them that their model is much, much bigger than the real molecule, which is so small that you need a special microscope to see it.

Hand the children one color of modeling compound, about the size of a walnut (adjust size to suit the amount of compound you have). Instruct them to roll the clay into a ball. Tell them this ball represents the oxygen atom.

Hand them the second color and instruct them to roll two balls, a little smaller than the first. These represent the hydrogen atoms.

When the hydrogen and oxygen atoms stick together, they make water, but they stick together in a certain way. The easiest way for children to picture this is to think of mouse ears. Tell them to imagine that the larger, oxygen atom is the mouse's head. The smaller, hydrogen atoms are the mouse's ears. Let them attach the ears to the head.

Place the molecule on a paper plate.

ACTIVITY FIVE: Exploring Water Pressure

Purpose

To explore the effects of water pressure

Materials

- half-gallon cartons
- duct tape
- scissors or phillips head screwdriver
- water
- funnel
- chalk
- table or chairs that can get wet

Preparation

This activity will be set up as an experiment station. Prepare the cartons by boring holes in one side with either the scissors or the screwdriver. Space the holes out, with one near the bottom, one near the top, and the one in the middle and make sure the holes are big enough for the water to flow through easily.

Cover the holes securely with tape and set the cartons on the table or chairs.

Just before the children arrive, fill the cartons with water.

Procedure

Ask the children if they have ever been in a swimming pool. Did they notice that if they swam to the bottom of the deep end that they felt more pressure on their ears (maybe their ears even hurt)? Tell them that water has weight and the deeper water is, the more it presses down. We call this water pressure.

Let the children experiment with the cartons. Take the tape off the holes in the water-filled cartons. As they explore, help them notice that the water that comes out of the bottom hole goes farther than the water from the top hole. Ask them if they can think why that is. (There is more water pushing down at the bottom hole. The greater pressure shoots the water farther.) As the water is depleted, you'll need to replenish it.

Challenge them to figure out how to make the water shoot the farthest and the closest.

Challenge them to experiment with different combinations of holes to figure out what difference it makes in how far the water will shoot. If you are set up on asphalt or concrete, they can use the chalk to mark where the water lands. (Alternately, mark an X on the pavement and challenge the kids to get the water to land on the X. They can use different combinations of holes and also different amounts of water.)

ACTIVITY SIX: Build a Dam (Like a Beaver)

Purpose

To learn how water can be controlled to change the environment

Materials

- lots of twigs and small sticks or coffee stirrers
- small stones
- dirt or modeling clay

- water
- disposable bowls
- plastic shoebox-size bins
- two buckets
- hand sanitizer
- picture of a beaver dam (optional)

Preparation

Make mud with the dirt and water and put in bowls.

Fill the buckets with water. One bucket will be for the dams and the other for getting mud off hands.

Procedure

Ask the children if they know what a dam is. Tell them that dams can be built to do different things, such as provide water for farmland or to make electricity. But all dams have one thing in common: they stop the flow of a river or stream.

Ask the children if they know who built the first dams. The beaver! The beaver is quite a clever engineer and can change the whole landscape with its dams.

In this activity, we are going to try to build dams similar to what a beaver builds to see if we can stop the flow of water.

Depending on how many bins you have, children can work in small groups or individually. Give each group or individual a bin, along with access to the sticks and twigs or coffee stirrers, small stones, and mud or modeling clay.

If you have a photo of a dam, show the children. Then instruct them to use the materials however they see fit to build a dam across the middle of their bin. Once the dam is completed, let them pour water on one side and see if their dam stops the flow of water to the other side.

While the children are working, you can talk with them about the importance of beaver dams. Dams create wetlands that attract fish, ducks, frogs, and other animals. Dams filter the water so that sediments and poisons don't pollute streams and the ocean. And dams can raise the groundwater upstream, which helps keep plants and animals alive during dry seasons.

When they are finished, have the children rinse their hands in the bucket of water and then use hand sanitizer or wash their hands in the sink with soap and water.

ACTIVITY SEVEN: Building Dams (Like an Engineer)

Purpose

To help the children begin to understand some basic dam structures

Materials

- long, shallow plastic bins or a sandbox
- sand
- water
- buckets
- craft sticks or unsharpened pencils
- poster board
- sticks
- stones
- cereal boxes
- scissors
- three containers for supplies
- scoop or cup
- book about dams, such as *How Are They Built? Dams* by Lynn M. Stone (Vero Beach, FL: Rourke Publishing, 2002)

Preparation

Prepare your riverbed by piling sand up in the bin on both sides, with the river bed running down the middle. Make the riverbed wide enough to challenge the children and keep the sand wet so it doesn't slide into the river. Or do this activity in a sandbox.

Prop one end up slightly so the river will flow.

Sort supplies into containers. In one container, put supplies for an arch dam: poster board and scissors. In the second container, put supplies for buttress dams: cereal boxes, craft sticks or pencils, and scissors. In the third container, put supplies for the embankment/gravity dam: sticks, stones, and sand.

Procedure

Tell the children that later they will be learning about a girl who lives in a country called Tajikistan. Tajikistan is a poor country, but they have one important resource—freshwater. By building dams, they are able to use this water to make electricity and to irrigate crops. In fact, the highest dam in the world, the Nurek Dam, is in Tajikistan.

Tell the children, "In this activity, you will explore some different types of dams—an arch dam, an embankment/gravity dam, and a buttress dam."

Show the children a picture of an arch dam. Tell them that the curved shape gives strength to the dam. If children want to build this type of dam, suggest that they first make a dam straight across the river and test how well it works, then make a dam that curves. Be sure they close any gaps on the bottom and sides with sand, but don't use so much sand that the sand is what is holding back the water.

Next show pictures of embankment dams and gravity dams. Tell the children that these dams use their heavy weight to resist the force of the water pushing against them. They are thicker and heavier than arch dams. If children want to try this type of dam, suggest they try building different shapes, such as the same thickness from top to bottom and then thicker at the bottom and thinner at the top.

Finally, show a picture of a buttress dam. Tell the children that these dams can be flat or curved. The important part is the buttresses supporting them on the downstream side. These buttresses push against the water that is pushing against the dam. If children want to try this kind of dam, suggest they begin by making a flat dam across the river without support, testing with water flow, then adding supports on the downstream side with craft sticks anchored in sand and leaning against the dam. Remind them to close gaps on the bottom and sides with sand, but not to use so much sand that it is the sand that is holding back the water.

Let the children experiment with different ideas in the riverbed. Once they have a dam constructed, they can pour water into the river and test the dam.

FUN FACT: THE HIGHEST DAM IN THE WORLD, THE NUREK DAM, IS IN TAJIKISTAN.

ACTIVITY EIGHT: Planting Seeds

Purpose

To mimic what Barfimoh, a girl from Tajikistan, does to help her family

Materials

- potting soil
- disposable cups or egg cartons
- any large seeds (beans grow quickly)
- scoop (can be a disposable cup)
- newspaper, if working indoors
- water
- plastic wrap
- tape
- permanent marker

Preparation

If you are using egg cartons, cut them into smaller sections. If you have enough cartons, you can cut them into two or four cup sections.

If working indoors, spread newspapers over your work area.

Procedure

Tell the children that later they will learn about a girl named Barfimoh, who lives in Tajikistan. One of her chores is to help the family plant seeds on their farm. So today, they are going to plant some seeds.

Give each child a cup or egg carton section and seeds. Write their names on the cups with the marker.

Let them scoop dirt into the cup and plant the seeds according to the directions on the package. Show them how to water the seeds without flooding the dirt.

Stretch plastic wrap over the cup and secure with tape. This will keep the seeds from drying out. The seeds should sprout in a few days' time.

ACTIVITY NINE: Fetching Water Relay

Purpose

To move water from one bucket to another

Materials

- four tubs
- two large coffee containers
- water
- large nail
- hammer

Preparation

Turn the coffee containers upside down and use the nail and hammer to make lots of holes in the bottom.

Place two tubs at each end of your relay field. Fill the tubs at one end with water.

Procedure

Tell the children that the purpose of the relay is to move as much water as they can from one bucket to the other. The relay will last until one of the full buckets is empty. At that time, whichever team has the most water in the second bucket wins.

Divide the children into two groups, evenly distributing older and younger children. Give the first child in each group a coffee container. Tell them to fill it with water from the first bucket, run to the other end, and dump (what is left) in the second bucket. Then they should run back to the start and hand the coffee container to the next child.

REGROUPING—STORY TIME

Book: *I Know the River Loves Me* by Maya Christina Gonzalez (San Francisco: Children's Book Press, 2009)

WHOLE GROUP ACTIVITIES

ACTIVITY ONE: Discussing the Country of the Day—Tajikistan

Purpose

To locate Tajikistan on the map and discover its annual rainfall

Materials

- map of continents
- two labels marked Tajikistan
- tape
- blue yarn, 20 inches long

Preparation

Make sure you know where Tajikistan is located.

Procedure

Say, "Today we are going to learn about a girl named Barfimoh, who lives in Tajikistan."

"Does anyone know what continent Tajikistan is in?" (It is in Asia, in the area better known as Central Asia.) "Where is Asia?" (Use the map hung up on the first day.) "Very good. Now, does anyone know where Tajikistan is?" Show the children the approximate location of Tajikistan and let a child attach the label with tape.

"Now who would like to guess how much rain falls every year in Tajikistan?" Give children a chance to answer. Tell children that Tajikistan is full of mountains, including some of the highest mountains in the world. The higher up a mountain you live, the less rain you get. But if you live in the capital city, Dushanbe, you'll get about 20 inches of rain each year. Let a child help you unroll the blue yarn and tape it to the wall, with the second Tajikistan label.

ACTIVITY TWO: Comparing Our Lives

Purpose

To compare the children's daily lives with that of a girl who lives in Tajikistan

Materials

- two hundred paper lunch bags
- large sheet of paper
- marker

Procedure

Ask the children how they get water in their house. (from a faucet) How would they get water if they didn't have a tap? (Give children a chance to respond. Possible answers include drawing water from a well, buying water from the store, getting water from a river. *Note:* If children suggest getting water from unsafe sources, point out to them that they should only drink water that has been cleaned, so ask their parents first.)

Tell the children that Barfimoh is a girl who lives in Tajikistan. In her village, there is no running water, so she and her sisters collect water from a spring at the bottom of a steep hill. They fill smaller buckets at the tap at the spring, then pour it into larger containers. (See the photo on page 39 of *Our World of Water*.)

Ask the children, "If you had to ride a donkey to the bottom of a steep hill to get water, would you use water differently than you do now?" Encourage them to think of all the ways they use water and write their answers on the large sheet of paper. Make sure you include flushing the toilet, taking a shower, taking a bath, washing dishes by hand, washing dishes in a dishwasher, washing laundry in the washing machine, brushing teeth.

Pass the paper lunch bags out to the children. Each bag has the volume of about half a gallon. Now, you and the children can look at how much water each of our daily activities uses. Begin with flushing the toilet. Tell the children that some toilets use less than two gallons of water. Ask the children how many lunch bags you need to equal two gallons if each bag is half a gallon. (Older elementary children may enjoy the math challenge.) Ask a child/children to open and bring to the front four lunch bags to illustrate the two gallons. Do this with each activity listed: running a dishwasher—5 gallons, washing dishes by hand—16 gallons, taking a shower—20 gallons, using the washing machine—30 gallons, taking a bath—37 gallons. Line them up to show how much all of these activities add up to. (*Note:* If the attention span of the group begins to wane, stop and use what you've done to help the children see that our daily activities use a lot of water.)

CONSERVATION TIP: CONSIDER FILLING A GALLON (OR EVEN HALF-GALLON) MILK JUG WITH WATER AND PLACING IT IN YOUR TOILET TANK TO CONSERVE WATER. OVER THE COURSE OF A YEAR, SEVERAL HUNDRED GALLONS OF WATER WILL BE CONSERVED.

Ask the kids to discuss whether they would like to bring that much water up a hill every day. How might they change their water usage to use as little as possible? Tell them that, because it takes a lot of work to get water to the house, Barfimoh must be careful not to use too much.

Since water is hard to get, Barfimoh's family collects rainwater from their roof. They use this water for the crops they grow on their farm. Does anyone remember from the activities what we call it when we collect water? (Water harvesting) Water harvesting is another way to conserve water.

Tell children that we are lucky in this country that most of the time we have all the clean water we need right at our fingertips. But it is important to remember that what we do can affect other people, so it is a good idea to learn to be careful about how much water we use.

CLOSING

Reviewing

- What fun thing did you learn about water today?
- What is "water harvesting"?
- What did you learn about Tajikistan?

PARTING PRAYER

May we always remember, O God, that water doesn't have to be used in baptism to be sacred or holy. All water is sacred, because you made it and it brings life to the whole world. So help us to always remember to respect the wonderful gift of water. Amen.

FIVE

Jesus Stills the Waves

SCRIPTURE TEXTS
Matthew 8:23–27

VERSE OF THE DAY
[Jesus] ordered . . . the waves to stop, and there was a great calm.
(Matthew 8:26, GNT)

PURPOSE OF THE LESSON
To explore different characteristics of water
and learn more about bodies of water

FOR THE LEADER—AN OPENING MEDITATION

Have you ever been on a lake in a small boat when a storm suddenly blew up, bringing a dark sky, violent winds, lightning, thunder, and threatening waves? It can be a frightening experience, even for adults. A beautiful, sunny, fun-filled day on the lake can turn ugly and unsettling in a matter of minutes. A setting known for offering life and recreation can become a place of crisis.

Today, many of our world's lakes are facing crisis, but a crisis of a different order. We have long known that many of our lakes have been so polluted that it is no longer safe to swim in them or eat the fish that come from them. But many are facing a crisis of yet a different sort—drying up. Shorelines are receding and these bodies of water that we have long taken for granted are endangered. In many cases, these lakes have served as primary water sources for entire towns, perhaps even large cities. Drought is one primary cause for the shrinking of many of our lakes. There isn't much we can do about that. But just as Jesus employed faith in responding to a lake in crisis in his own time, we can let our faith lead us in our efforts at conservation and careful use of water and respect for our own lakes facing crisis today.

GATHERING TIME

Welcome the children back. Ask what they remember about the last lesson. (Possible responses include water molecules, Jesus' baptism, small group activities, and Tajikistan.)

Say, "Today we are going to learn about where our water goes after it rains, hear a Bible story about a rough boat ride, do some more fun activities, and learn what it's like to live in a country called Mauritania."

"Let's start with our water song." (Or use the alternate hymn.)

Gathering Music

"Itsy, Bitsy Raindrops" (Words by Dot Keller; tune: "Itsy, Bitsy Spider")

Itsy, bitsy raindrops are falling all around.
On the streets and sidewalks and on the sun-baked ground.
Making green our flowers and quenching thirsty trees.
Itsy, bitsy raindrops are falling down on me.

Or sing "I've Got Peace Like a River" (*The New Century Hymnal* #478).

WHOLE GROUP ACTIVITY
Where in the World Is Your Water Drop?

Purpose

To demonstrate how long water spends in various places on and above the earth

Materials

- adding machine tape
- red, blue, green, and yellow crayons

- tape measure
- ruler (if tape measure doesn't have metric)
- scissors
- pencil

Preparation

For this activity, you'll divide your large group into small groups of three to four children. Cut one strip of adding machine tape that is 100 inches long for each group and one for yourself.

Color your strip as follows: 98 inches blue for the ocean; 1 millimeter green for the freshwater, such as rivers; about 2 inches red for ice; and about half a millimeter yellow for the atmosphere.

Procedure

Divide your large group into smaller groups of three to four children. Make sure each group has an adult available to help them understand the activity.

Say, "Tomorrow we will learn where we can find water on the earth. Can anyone guess?" (Water is in the ocean, in ice, and in lakes, rivers, streams and other freshwater sources) "We already learned from the water cycle that water isn't always on the earth. Sometimes it's up in the air.

"If you could follow a water drop for a hundred years, you would discover that it spends time in these four places: some time in the ocean, some time locked in ice, some time in freshwater such as rivers, and some time in the air."

Give each group a strip of adding machine tape, pencil, and crayons. Tell them that the paper is 100 inches long and represents one hundred years. If you like, you can help them find the halfway point and mark this as fifty years, then they can find the quarter points and mark them as twenty-five and seventy-five years.

Tell them to imagine a water drop beginning a hundred-year journey. It will start life in the atmosphere, then it will fall to earth and become part of a glacier. Then it will melt and flow into a river and eventually find itself in the ocean. How long do they think the drop will spend in each of these four places?

Let them use a different color crayon for each place the water drop will be and color the adding machine tape to show how much time is spent in each place. For example,

they can choose blue to represent the ocean. If they think the water drop is in the ocean for fifty years, they can color half of the paper strip blue.

After the groups have had a chance to color in their answers, let them share. Then share the strip you prepared ahead of time. Tell them that the water drop will spend less than a week in the atmosphere, twenty months (almost two years) as ice, about two weeks as fresh liquid water (lakes and rivers), and about ninety-eight years in the ocean.

STUDYING

Verse of the Day

Jesus "ordered . . . the waves to stop, and there was a great calm." (Matthew 8:26 GNT)

Bible Story: Matthew 8:23–27 (paraphrased)

Jesus spent a lot of time around the lake. Sometimes he crossed the lake in a boat. One day Jesus got into a boat to cross the lake, and some of his disciples were in the boat with him. All of a sudden, a terrible storm came up while they were out in the lake. The waves were getting fierce. The little boat was being tossed about. Water was splashing over the sides of the boat. It looked as though the boat was in danger of sinking. But while the storm was raging, Jesus was taking a nap.

The disciples were terrified! They shook Jesus to wake him up and cried, "Wake up, Jesus! Do something to save us. We are about to be thrown out of the boat and drowned!"

"Don't be afraid," Jesus said. "Have a little faith." Then Jesus stood up and waved his hand and told the storm to die down and ordered the waves to become calm. And they did.

The disciples were amazed. "Who is this man?" they wondered. "Even the winds and the waves listen to him!"

Question and Discussion Time

1. Have you ever ridden in a boat on a lake or ocean?

2. How would you feel if you were in a small boat on the lake when a storm arose and the waves started splashing water into the boat?

3. If you were in the boat during a storm, whom would you want in the boat with you? (someone strong who could bring the boat safely to the shore, a sailor)

4. What can help us during those times when we are afraid? (faith, prayer, courage, remembering we are not alone)

5. Why do you think Jesus' followers have found courage to face frightening situations?

6. Could this story have meaning for us for all kinds of situations in our lives when we might be afraid?

EXPLORING — SMALL GROUP ACTIVITIES

Note: Activity One needs time, so set it up while the children are still in the whole group. You will come back to it when you discuss the country of the day.

ACTIVITY ONE: Cooling Water without Electricity

Purpose

To introduce children to the idea that not all people have electricity to cool their water and food and to show them a method for cooling that doesn't use electricity

Materials

- nine plastic cups
- six unglazed clay pots, bigger than the cups
- sand
- bucket of water
- five cloths big enough to cover the pots
- two cloths big enough to wrap around a pot
- seven thermometers that will fit in the cups

- three bowls
- duct tape

Procedure

Ask the children how they keep water and other drinks cold at their house. (If they mention putting water in a cooler with ice, ask them how they make ice.) A refrigerator and freezer are very useful, but both require electricity to work. In some parts of the world, people do not have electricity in their homes, but they still need to keep water cool, and also their food. One way of doing this is with clay pots.

Divide the children into six groups with a teenage or adult helper in each group.

Each group will set up a slightly different experiment and will compare results at the end of small group time. Set one cup of water aside with a thermometer in it. This will be your control; it will show the temperature of the water without a clay pot. Now, give each group their supplies and instructions:

Group One receives a pot, cup of water, a piece of tape and a thermometer. First they need to dip the pot in the bucket of water to thoroughly wet it and tape up the hole in the bottom of the pot. Then they need to set the thermometer in the cup and turn the pot over on top of it.

Group Two receives a pot, cup of water, thermometer, and cloth (to cover the pot). First they need to soak the pot in the bucket of water to thoroughly wet it, then set the cup in the pot with the thermometer in the cup. Then cover the pot with the cloth.

Group Three receives a pot, a bowl of sand, cup of water, thermometer, and a cloth (to cover the pot). They are to set the cup in the pot and pack the sand between the cup and the pot. Then they will put the thermometer in the cup and cover the top of the pot with the dry cloth.

Group Four receives a pot, a bowl of sand, two cups of water, thermometer, and cloth (to cover the pot). They are to set one of the cups in the pot, and pack the sand between the cup and the pot. Then they will pour the water from the second cup onto the sand, soaking it thoroughly, getting more water from the bucket, if needed. Then they will put the thermometer in the cup and cover the pot with the cloth.

Group Five receives a pot, a cup of water, a large cloth, and a thermometer. They are to put the thermometer in the cup and turn the pot over on the cup. Then soak the large cloth in the bucket, squeeze it so it is not too drippy, and wrap it around the pot.

Group Six receives a pot, a bowl of sand, two cups of water, the remaining two cloths, and a thermometer. They are to put the thermometer in one of the cups and set it in the pot, then pack the sand between the cup and the pot. Then they will pour the water from the second cup onto the sand, soaking it thoroughly, getting more water from the bucket, if needed. Next, they will soak the large cloth, squeeze it so it is not too drippy, and wrap it around the pot. Finally, they will lay the smaller cloth on top of the pot.

Once the pots are prepared, set them outside, so that all are exposed to the same light and temperature. You will return to the pots after small group time.

Optional: If you would like to experiment further, you can make identical pot setups and put each pot in a different type of environment, for example, in the shade and in the sun. Compare how the environment affects the pots' ability to cool the water.

Alternative: If your group would prefer a simpler version, they can set up only one or two of the variations.

ACTIVITY TWO: Crayon Resist Painting

Purpose

To reinforce the Bible story

Materials

- glossy paper or card stock
- crayons, especially white
- watercolor paints
- paintbrushes
- small disposable cups
- water
- pencil or pen

Procedure

Ask the children what the Bible story was about today. Ask them if they have ever been to a lake. Lakes are homes to many animals. What kinds of animals might you find in a lake?

Give the children each a piece of paper and access to the crayons. You may want to write their names on the back of the paper before they start. Then tell them to draw a picture, either of the Bible story or of a lake with some of the animals they mentioned. They will need to push fairly hard on the crayons so their lines are thick. This will make the finished product look better. Encourage them to use white crayon, which will show up after the picture is painted.

As a child finishes, give him or her a paintbrush, a cup of water, and access to watercolor paints. Instruct them to dip the brush first in the water and then the paint, and to paint over the crayon, covering the whole page. The final product will look better if they don't get the paint too wet and brush lightly.

ACTIVITY THREE: Making Waves

Purpose

To help children understand how a wave moves

Materials

- plastic bins, shoebox size or larger
- water
- straws
- spoons
- corks (or other small items that float)

Procedure

Set up several bins with water, so several children can experiment at the same time. Place a cork in each bin. Before the children try the activity, make sure the water is still.

Recall the Bible story with the children. Ask them why the disciples were afraid. (A storm came and waves were breaking into the boat.) Have they ever been to the ocean or a lake and seen waves? If you look at waves, it seems that the water is moving, doesn't it. But really, the water isn't moving very far at all, mostly up and down.

Let each child test this by using a straw to blow across the water in one of the bins. The force of the wind they create will push the cork across the water.

Now have the children use the spoon to make waves by dipping the spoon in and out of the water. The wave travels to the other side of the bin, but the cork stays mostly in the same place.

ACTIVITY FOUR: Fish Kites (especially for younger children)

Purpose

To make a colorful kite while learning that fish are an important food source for people who live near the ocean

Materials

- construction paper (9 x 12 inches)
- thin dowel rods or paper towel tubes
- scissors
- markers
- glitter (optional)
- sequins (optional)
- glue sticks (optional)
- hole punch
- yarn

Procedure

Tell the children that in some places, people depend on food that comes from the ocean, such as fish. That is one reason why it is important to keep our oceans clean, so that the food people eat is also clean.

To help us remember, let's make a kind of kite shaped like a fish.

Give each child a piece of construction paper, a marker, and scissors, and instruct them to draw and cut out a fish shape.

(Optional) Use the markers, glitter, sequins, and glue sticks to decorate the fish. Be careful that the fish does not get too heavy.

Punch a hole about where the mouth should be and thread a length of yarn through it. One and a half feet should be a good length. Tie one end to the fish and the other end to the dowel rod. (Optional: If you prefer, tie the yarn to a paper towel tube.)

The children can "fly" their fish by waving the rod. Be careful to supervise children with the sticks.

> **CONSERVATION TIP:** YOU CAN HELP PROTECT MARINE WILDLIFE EVEN IF YOU LIVE FAR FROM THE BEACH. REMEMBER THAT STORM DRAINS ON YOUR STREET EMPTY INTO STREAMS AND RIVERS, AND EVENTUALLY THE OCEAN, SO WE SHOULD KEEP CHEMICALS AND TRASH OUT.

ACTIVITY FIVE: Sailboats

Purpose

To reinforce the Bible story by reminding children of the boat on the lake

Materials

- foam food trays (CAUTION: Do not use meat trays.)
- disposable foam bowls
- tape
- scraps of packaging foam
- disposable three ounce cups
- drinking straws
- plastic grocery bags (CAUTION: Watch children closely with plastic bags so that they do not put them over their faces.)
- scrap paper
- scissors
- pencil
- kiddie pool
- water

Preparation

Fill the kiddie pool about halfway with water. (CAUTION: Have an adult near the pool at all times when children are present.)

You can precut materials, especially if you are working with younger children. Cut straws so that one piece is one to two inches longer than the other. Cut two- to two-and-a-half-inch squares from the plastic bags and paper. For older children, leave the supplies uncut so they can decide for themselves what to do.

Procedure

Note: The following steps are suggestions for younger children. Older children can be given supplies to create on their own.

Either use a foam tray or a disposable bowl. The tray can be cut, if desired.

Take two pieces of straw, one larger than the other. Cross them so that the horizontal straw is about a third of the way from the top of the vertical straw. Tape them together.

Insert the bottom of the vertical straw in a piece of packaging foam and tape it to the tray or bowl. Alternately, poke a hole in the bottom of a three-ounce cup and stick the straw in there. Secure with tape.

Make a sail by cutting a square from a plastic bag or paper. (Or use a precut square.) Turn the square on the diagonal and tape each corner to the end of a straw. It will look something like a kite when you are done.

Set the boat in the water and blow on the sail or fan it with a piece of cardboard. How well does it float and move? Can you think of ways to make it better? Try another idea!

ACTIVITY SIX: Ocean in a Bottle

Purpose

To mimic the ocean, beside which the child of the day lives

Materials

- plastic drinking bottles with lids, labels removed
- funnels
- blue food dye
- cooking oil
- water
- pitcher

- duct tape
- tiny shells (optional)
- birthday candles, cut in half (optional)
- sand (optional)

Procedure

Help the children use the funnel to fill the bottle about half full of oil. Add an equal amount of water and a few drops of food dye. (Supervise the dye carefully to avoid staining clothes.)

Add shells, sand, and birthday candles if you like. (The candles will float between the oil and water.)

Screw the lid on and tape securely with the duct tape. (Turn it upside down to make sure there are no leaks.)

Lay the bottle on its side to see the ocean.

ACTIVITY SEVEN: Washing Your Hands

Purpose

To experience how an ordinary activity changes when water is in short supply

Materials

- plastic pitchers or cups
- plastic bowls
- liquid soap
- vegetable shortening
- water
- towels

Procedure

Have the children work in pairs and take turns washing their hands.

Ask the children when they should wash their hands (such as before eating). Ask them how they usually wash their hands (using a faucet at a sink). Point out that it's easy for us to wash our hands because we have plenty of water available. But in some parts of the world, water is hard to come by. People have to be very careful how they use it or they will run out. The child we will learn about today lives in such a country. Let's learn to wash our hands the way she washes hers.

Challenge each pair to use as little water as possible and still get their hands clean. First, one of the pair should get his or her hands a little greasy with the shortening. Then he or she should clean hands, using the soap and letting the second child pour water from the pitcher over the bowl. They can note how much water is in the bowl and strive to use less the second time.

Note: Since the used water will have soap in it, pour it down a drain rather than on the ground.

ACTIVITY EIGHT: How Do Submarines Work? (for older children)

Purpose

To understand how submarines can float and sink

Materials

- tall, clear, plastic glasses
- water
- vinegar
- baking soda
- raisins
- tablespoon
- half teaspoon

Procedure

Ask the children if they know what a submarine is. Have they ever wondered how a submarine can sink, then float, then sink again? They will do an experiment to find out.

Fill the glass with water.

Add a few raisins to the glass. What happens to them? (They sink.)

Use the tablespoon to add three tablespoons of vinegar to the water.

Add half a teaspoon of baking soda to the glass. What happens? (Bubbles!)

Watch the raisins. What happens to them? (They float to the surface.) Why do they float? (Because the bubbles that attach to the raisins are filled with air and because air is lighter than water, the raisins float.) What happens when the raisins reach the surface? (The bubbles pop and the raisins sink.) If the reaction slows down, you can add a bit more baking soda.

Tell the children that a submarine works in a similar way. A submarine has tanks called ballast tanks. When the submarine wants to sink, the tanks fill with seawater, which makes the submarine heavy. When the submarine wants to float, the seawater is pushed out of the tanks and air is pushed in.

ACTIVITY NINE: How Do Submarines Work? (for younger children)

Purpose

To use a simple activity to show why a submarine floats or sinks

Materials

- plastic cups
- container (large enough for several children to use)
- water

Procedure

Fill the container with water.

Give the children each a plastic cup and show them how to hold the cup upside down over the water. Make sure the cups are not tilted.

Tell them to push the cups into the water. They will have to push hard because the cups are filled with air. Once they get the cups at least partially underwater, they can let go. The cup will pop back to the surface.

Next, show the children how to push the cup into the water at an angle so that water fills the cup. Without much effort, the cup will sink to the bottom.

Tell the children that a submarine works this way. A submarine has tanks called ballast tanks. When the submarine wants to sink, the tanks fill with seawater, which makes the submarine heavy. When the submarine wants to float, the seawater is pushed out of the tanks and air is pushed in.

ACTIVITY TEN: How Waves Break up a Shore

Purpose

To explore water's effects on the landscape

Materials

- several plastic bins, at least two feet long
- modeling clay
- walnut size rocks
- sand

- water
- dustpan or cardboard, no wider than the width of the bin
- bucket

Procedure

Tell the children that water is very strong and can change the shape of the land. Ask if any of them have been to the beach. What did they think about the waves? Do they know what causes ocean waves? (the pull of the moon as it circles the Earth)

Tell them that waves can change the way the coast looks. Show them photos from a book.

Tell them that they are going to make a shoreline and then see how the waves change the look of it. You can let children work individually or in small groups. Give each child or group a plastic bin, some modeling clay, and several rocks.

First they should place several small bits of clay at one end of the bin, then firmly press rocks into the clay.

They should then cover the rocks with sand until they are hidden. The sand should take up about half the tray. Have the children pour water into the other half.

To make waves, children can use the dustpan or cardboard and sweep it back and forth in the water so the water washes on the sand. Ask them, "What happens to the sand? How is the shoreline changed?"

ACTIVITY ELEVEN: Fishing Relay

Purpose

To "fish for their supper"

Materials

- poster board or card stock
- paper clips
- doughnut magnets
- yardsticks
- string
- scissors

- tape
- two containers
- two baskets

Preparation

Cut fish shapes from the poster board or card stock, each three to four inches long, and attach a paper clip to each one.

Make fishing rods by tying or taping string to the yardsticks and tying the free end to the magnets. Set the fish in the containers.

Set the containers, the baskets, and the fishing rods at one end of the relay course.

Procedure

Remind the children that people who live near the ocean eat a lot of seafood. In this relay, they are going to go fishing.

Divide the children into teams and line them up at the end opposite the fish. Tell the children that they need to run to the other end, use the fishing rod to get a fish from the container and put it in the basket. Once they have done so, they are to set the fishing rod down and run back to the start.

The first group to get all their fish from the container to the basket wins.

REGROUPING — STORY TIME

Book: *River Story* by Meredith Hooper (Cambridge, MA: Candlewick Press, 2000).

WHOLE GROUP ACTIVITIES

ACTIVITY ONE: Discussing the Country of the Day—Mauritania

Purpose

To locate Mauritania on the map and discover its annual rainfall

Materials

- map of continents
- two labels marked Mauritania

- tape
- blue yarn, six inches long
- large sheet of paper

Preparation

Make sure you know where Mauritania is located.

If you like, tape the large sheet of paper to the wall.

Procedure

After story time, draw children's attention to the world map that was assembled during Lesson One. Remind them that they have been learning about rainfall in different countries around the world. Today, they will look at the country of Mauritania.

Show them the Mauritania label and ask if anyone knows where it belongs. If no one knows, call on a child to help you attach it to the proper place. Ask the children which continent Mauritania is on (Africa). Point out that the country lies on the ocean.

Tell the children that today they are going to learn a little about a girl named Khadija, who lives in Mauritania. But first, ask if anyone would like to guess how much rainfall Mauritania gets in one year. Give the children a chance to guess and allow the one who guesses the closest to help you attach the yarn next to the previous yarns. As you are attaching the yarn, tell the children that the city where Khadija lives gets about six inches of rain each year.

ACTIVITY TWO: Comparing Our Lives

Purpose

To learn how daily life would be different if you lived in a country without much rain

Materials

- marker
- six clay pots set up before Small Group time
- thermometer

Procedure

Ask the children to brainstorm with you how their lives might be different if they lived in a country that didn't get much rain. Write their responses on the large sheet of paper.

If someone mentioned conserving water, point out that this is something Khadija must be very careful about. People in her country have to be careful not to use too much water. Ask the children if they practiced washing their hands during Small Group time. Were they able to use just a little bit of water to get their hands clean? (Allow time for responses.) This is how Khadija washes her hands every day. (Show the photo of Khadija washing her hands from the book *Our World of Water*, page 15.)

If someone mentioned reusing water, point out that this is also something Khadija does. The water that is used to wash the rice is reused to water the sheep. And the water that drips from the storage pot is caught and used to water the trees. (Show the photo of Khadija watering the tree on page 16 of *Our World of Water*.)

Tell the children that although many people in Mauritania do not have running water in their homes, Khadija's family does have one tap in their house and they store the water from it in a large clay pot. Say, "Let's look at the experiment we set up earlier. Remember that we wanted to find out if putting water in the clay pots would help cool the water. Now we are going to find out."

Check the water temperature in each pot. Compare the temperature with the temperature of the water that was not in a clay pot. Is there a difference? Which pot worked best for cooling the water? Ask, "Are clay pots a good way to cool water if you don't have a refrigerator?" (*Note:* Cheap thermometers are not always accurate and two thermometers can give two different readings. If this is the case for you, use one thermometer to measure the water in each cup. This will take more time, so you may want someone to do this ahead of time.)

Recap by saying that your daily life is different if you live in a place that doesn't get much water. And even if you are lucky to live in a place with plenty of clean water, you can still learn some good habits from Khadija about carefully using what you have.

CLOSING

Reviewing

- What thing that you learned today surprised you the most?
- Did you know that many children in the world have a much more difficult time acquiring and stretching their use of water?
- What are some ways that your family might stretch your use of water, using it more than once?

PARTING PRAYER

Jesus, who quieted the stormy waves: Be with us when we are frightened. Help us to be brave and remember that we are not alone when we are scared, but there are others who are with us to help us. Amen.

SIX

Gathering at the Community Well

SCRIPTURE TEXTS
John 4:5–11, 13–15, 25–26, 28–30, 39–40

FOCUS OF THE DAY
Wells provide life-giving water.

PURPOSE OF THE LESSON
*To learn about the importance of community wells,
as well as the importance of keeping water clean,
and ways that dirty water can be made clean
and usable again*

FOR THE LEADER—AN OPENING MEDITATION

People of every age and place have had their community gathering places. I am guessing that in Jesus' day the community well was such a place—the local gathering spot where people gathered to loaf, socialize, gossip, and tell big tales.

Of course, the *literal* community well has something everyone needs. Water. Refreshing, life-giving water. Water is the thing that we need more than anything else in life. One can live several weeks without food, but only a few days without water. We put a high premium on water. Have you ever stopped to think that many of us who buy bottled water pay more per gallon for it than we do for gasoline for our automobiles? Water is the earth's most precious resource, more precious than silver, gold, or platinum.

Yet our world is approaching a state of crisis in regards to the availability of clean drinking water. Some Southern and Western states in our country have in the past and certainly will in the future face severe water shortages.

But even worse is the situation in other countries of the world where water supplies are drying up completely. In some places, villagers have to walk for miles to find water for drinking and cooking. Some scientists warn that some countries are in real danger of being without water completely in a decade or two. So from a social justice standpoint, there is a real need for all of us to be careful about the water we use and waste. Is it possible that the water we use in this part of the country or world affects the water supply in other parts of the country or world? We will have to let scientists answer that question.

At any rate, it is important that today's story unfolds by a historic community well that provides the thing most necessary for human survival. And when people gather at the community well, as did Jesus and the woman of Samaria, it is something of significance. The community well stands as a living reality, and as a symbol, of that which everyone needs, that which gives life to the world.

In the end, we all come to the same community wells in search of the same things. It may be something as earthly as H_2O, life-giving water. But in a deeper, spiritual sense, we all are searching for that life-giving spiritual water and a sense of community.

GATHERING TIME

Welcome the children back for this last lesson. Tell them how glad you are that they have been a part of this VBS, camp, or other event. Ask them what they remember about the last lesson. (Possible responses include where water goes, Jesus' calming the water, small group activities, and Mauritania.)

Say, "Today, we're going to learn about the water we use, hear a Bible story about Jesus' making a friend, do some fun activities, and learn what it's like to live in a country called Ethiopia."

"First, let's sing our water song one more time." (Or use the alternate hymn.)

Gathering Music

"Itsy, Bitsy Raindrops" (Words by Dot Keller; tune: "Itsy, Bitsy Spider")

Itsy-bitsy raindrops are falling all around.
On the streets and sidewalks and on the sun-baked ground.

Making green our flowers and quenching thirsty trees.
Itsy, bitsy raindrops are falling down on me.

Or sing "With Joy Draw Water" (*The New Century Hymnal* #109).

Whole Group Activity
Water, Water, Everywhere! What Can I Drink?

Purpose

To make children aware of how much of the Earth's water is available to use

Materials

Note: You will need a set of these supplies for each small group and for the leader.

- four one-liter bottles with lids
- measuring cup with metric markings
- bucket of water
- three sheets of paper
- tape
- permanent marker
- funnel

Preparation

Tape the earth covered with the blue raindrops on the wall (from Lesson One).

For each small group, fill a one-liter bottle with 1000 ml of water and screw on the lid.

Procedure

Use the earth with raindrops to remind the children that there is a lot of water on earth. Explain to them that although there is a lot of water on Earth, not all of it is okay for us to drink. Do they remember what is in ocean water? (salt) So we call that saltwater, and it's not good for us to drink. Other water doesn't have salt and we call that . . . (wait for an answer) . . . fresh. Freshwater is okay for us to drink if it's clean.

Ask the children where they think water is found on earth. Listen to the children's answers, then write them on one of three pieces of blank paper. On one paper, write any answers that are saltwater sources, on another, write freshwater sources that are unlocked (not frozen), and on the last, write locked (frozen) sources. For example, on the first sheet you may have oceans, seas, Great Salt Lake. On the second, you may have ponds, lakes, rivers, streams, puddles. On the last, you may have glaciers, ice caps. After the kids have given their answers, you can label the sheets: Ask the kids what the water sources on the first sheet have in common. (They are all salty.) Write saltwater on that sheet. Ask them what the water sources on the second sheet have in common. (They are freshwater.) Write freshwater on that sheet. Ask them what the water sources on the third sheet have in common. (They are frozen.) Write locked on that sheet. Explain that we call frozen water locked because we cannot use it.

If you haven't already, you can divide your large group into smaller groups. It would be beneficial if each group has an adult or teenager to help.

Give each group three empty bottles with lids, a marker, a funnel, and a measuring cup. Ask them to label the bottles saltwater, freshwater, and locked water.

Next, give each group a filled bottle. Tell them that the water in the bottle stands for all the water on the earth. They need to divide the water (with help and a funnel) into the three empty bottles. So, first, they need to guess how much water is fresh, how much is salty, and how much is locked. *Note:* Let the children decide for themselves.

Once they have finished filling their bottles (make sure the lids are on), it will be your turn to fill your bottles. Fill the measuring cup with 970 ml of water. Ask students if they think this represents the saltwater, freshwater, or locked water. Pour into the bottle labeled saltwater, using a funnel. Write 97% on the saltwater sheet taped to the wall—that's how much of our water is saltwater.

Fill measuring cup with 20 ml of water. Ask whether it represents freshwater or locked water. Pour into the bottle labeled locked water. Write 2% on locked water sheet. This is how much of our water is locked water.

Pour the rest of the water into the bottle marked freshwater. This is about 10 ml of water. Write 1% on the label. Students probably won't really understand the percentages, but will get a better idea by looking at how much water is in bottles. This is how much of all the water on the earth that is available for us to drink.

Were the children surprised by this? Allow time for the children to comment on this activity and what they discovered.

CONSERVATION TIP: A DRIPPING FAUCET CAN WASTE UP
TO TWENTY GALLONS OF WATER A DAY.

STUDYING

Focus of the Day

Wells provide life-giving water.

Bible Story: John 4:5–11, 13–15, 25–26, 28–30, 39–40 (paraphrased and summarized)

One day when Jesus was traveling, he came to a village named Sychar and sat down by the community well. The community well was where people in the village gathered to draw their water. Jesus was tired out by the trip, and he was very thirsty. It was about noon, so the sun was high up in the sky and very hot.

A Samaritan woman came to the well to draw some water. Jesus asked her to give him a drink of water.

The woman was shocked, and she said to him, "But you are a Jew, and I am a Samaritan—and I'm a woman! Why would you ask me for a drink of water?" (You see, Jews and Samaritans did not eat from the same bowls or drink from the same cups.)

Jesus and the woman had a long conversation. Jesus talked to the woman about her life, about God, and about worshiping God.

The woman was so excited about her newfound friend, Jesus, that she dropped her water jar on the ground and ran back into the village to tell her friends and neighbors. Her friends and neighbors came from the village to the well so they could meet Jesus, too.

After the woman's neighbors got to know Jesus, they begged him to come to their village and stay with them. So Jesus did; he stayed and visited with and taught the people of Sychar for two days. And it all happened because Jesus and a woman became friends at the community well.

Question and Discussion Time

1. Have you ever seen a well?

2. Have you ever seen someone draw water from a well?

3. What do you think makes village wells so important? (Everyone depends on the water the well provides; the well can be a village gathering place.)

4. Why is it so important to protect the community well? (The water needs to be kept clean, pure, and free of contamination.)

5. What might we do to help a community or village have a well or clean drinking water? (Collect money for digging a well, or collect money for clean water filters.)

EXPLORING—SMALL GROUP ACTIVITIES

Note: Since this is the last day, you can use up leftover supplies by repeating activities from earlier lessons.

ACTIVITY ONE: Making Dirty Water Clean

Purpose

To use the capillary property of water to filter dirty water
    CAUTION: Do not allow children to drink filtered water.

Materials

- paper towels
- cups, plastic or disposable
- dirt
- water
- books
- plastic grocery bags

Preparation

Cut the paper towel into strips one inch wide and as long as you need in order to reach from the top cup to the bottom cup.

Procedure

Note: You don't need to explain the science behind the capillary action of water, but you can point out to the children how the water climbs up the paper towel. This same action is how water gets from the roots of a plant up to the rest of the plant.

Let children pour some water into a cup and stir in a bit of dirt.

Stack several books together inside the plastic bag to protect them. Set the cup of dirty water on top of the books and an empty cup next to the stack.

Put one end of the paper towel strip into the dirty water and the other end into the dry cup. This will take a while, so let children move on to another activity and check back periodically.

When the children check back, talk with them about what happened: the water traveled along the paper towel and dripped into the empty cup, leaving the dirt behind. CAUTION: The filtered water will not be clean enough to drink. Supervise children so they don't drink it.

ACTIVITY TWO: Grinding Corn

Purpose

To experience grinding corn, similar to what the child of the day does

Materials

- corn seeds
- cutting boards
- rolling pins or large, smooth rocks
- towels
- cornmeal (just enough to show the children what it is)

Procedure

Tell the children that in some parts of the world, people can't run to the store to buy food; they have to grow and prepare their own. Let's find out what that's like.

Show the children the cornmeal and ask if they know what it is. What kind of things can we make from cornmeal? Tell them that you bought your cornmeal at the store, but in some places, people have to grow their own corn, or buy corn, and then make their own meal. Children will help grind the corn into meal.

Give each child a cutting board, if you are inside. They can use pavement if they are outside. Then give them a few corn seeds and a rolling pin or large, smooth rock.

Instruct them to cover the seeds with the towel. This helps prevent pieces of corn from hitting a child. Next, they can try to grind them with the rolling pin or rock. Do not allow the children to hit the seeds, as this could damage the rolling pins or produce splinters that could harm the children.

ACTIVITY THREE: Build an Aquifer

Purpose

To help children understand what groundwater is and where wells get their water

Materials

- clear, plastic disposable cups
- modeling clay
- gravel
- soil
- bucket with water
- three-ounce disposable cups
- wooden skewer or pencil
- food coloring
- sponges
- saucers
- straws

Preparation

Use the skewer or pencil to poke lots of tiny holes in the bottom of some of the disposable cups. You will also need some cups without holes.

Procedure

Ask the children if they know what groundwater is. Explain that groundwater is simply water that is under the ground. (Water in lakes and such is called surface water.) Do they know how the water gets under the ground? When it rains, the water soaks into the ground and goes through the rocks and sand and soil until it gets to a point where the ground is filled with water. Sometimes the water soaks down a long way, but sometimes it stops near the surface. If there is a lot of water under the ground, we call this an aquifer.

Do you know what groundwater can be used for? Groundwater can be used for drinking. Well water is water that comes from an aquifer. Groundwater can also be used to water crops.

Ask the children how they think the water is stored underground. Do they think there is a big empty space? Tell them that there are rocks and other sediment that have holes where the water seeps in and is stored.

Give each child a sponge and a small cup with holes poked in the bottom. Let them scoop water from the bucket and hold it over the sponge. Tell them that the water is like the rain. What is happening to the rain? (It is soaking into the sponge.) Tell them that some rocks are sort of like the sponge and have tiny holes that can hold water.

Next, tell the children that they are going to build a model aquifer. Give each child a clear cup and access to the clay, gravel and soil. Tell them to layer each in the cup, beginning with the clay, adding at least an inch of gravel, and finishing with the soil.

When they are ready, give each child a cup without holes and add water and a drop or two of food coloring. Also give them a cup with holes and instruct them to hold that cup over the cup with the soil and pour the dyed water into it. This is rain. Watch where the water collects. This models how water collects under the ground in an aquifer.

After the water has collected in the gravel, the children can "build a well" by inserting a straw through the dirt and into the gravel. Tell them to cover the top of the straw with a finger and pull it out. There should be water in the straw. Wells draw their water from groundwater, similar to this.

ACTIVITY FOUR: Make Your Own Water Filter

Purpose

To introduce children to the idea that water can be polluted and needs to be filtered before it is safe to drink

CAUTION: Do not allow children to drink the filtered water.

Note: This activity will work for younger children with more guidance from an adult. You may wish to select one or two filter materials, rather than have so many choices.

Materials

- plastic bottles (16-ounce or larger)
- cotton balls
- sand
- gravel
- activated carbon (optional)
- food dye
- soil
- cooking oil
- scraps of paper
- water
- disposable cups
- two bins or boxes

Preparation

Cut the bottles in half. You will need both halves.

Put the filter materials in one box: cotton balls, sand, gravel, and activated carbon. Put the pollutants in another box: food dye, soil, cooking oil, scraps of paper.

Procedure

Tell the children that sometimes water gets polluted (make sure they understand this term) and it must be cleaned before we can drink it. Water can be polluted by big things like dirt and trash, and it can be polluted by things that are too small to see. So we need different types of filters to get rid of the different things that make the water dirty.

Tell the children they are going to make their own water filters.

Give each child the top half of a bottle. Show them the materials in the first box and tell them these are the materials they'll use to make the filters. They are to select which ones they want to use, how much of each to use, and the order in which to layer them in the bottle. Tell them to begin by placing the cotton balls in the mouth of the filter. Then they can choose what else to use and how to use it. Challenge them to select just one or two materials.

Once they have their filters layered, they can set the bottle top in a bottom half. The filtered water will pool in the bottom.

Now they need to make some dirty water. Give them a cup of water and show them the materials in the second box. Tell them to select one, some, or all, and add them to the water. Once their water is dirty, they can pour it into the filter. It may take a while for it to come out the other end.

How did their filter work? If the water still looks dirty, challenge them to clean out the bottle and try again with different materials, different amounts of materials, and/or a different order of layering the materials.

CAUTION: Tell the children not to drink the water. Even if it looks clean, microbes can still be present.

ACTIVITY FIVE: Playing Jacks

Purpose

To learn a game similar to one that children play in Ethiopia

Materials

- small bouncy balls
- small rocks or beans

Procedure

Tell the children that in Ethiopia children play a game called toki, which is similar to jacks.

Spread the rocks or beans on the ground. Show the children how to bounce the ball, scoop up rocks, and then catch the ball before it hits the ground again.

They can challenge themselves to pick up one rock on the ball's first bounce, two rocks on the second bounce, and so forth.

ACTIVITY SIX: Play Dough Animals

Purpose

To make animals from play dough, to imitate what a child in Ethiopia might do for fun

Materials

- homemade play dough (recipe, p. 29, "Preparation")
- index cards
- marker

Procedure

Tell the children that if they lived in a country called Ethiopia, which is all the way in Africa, they might not have the kinds of toys and electronic gadgets that they do here. But they would still find ways to have fun. One thing children there like to do is use clay from the earth to make little animal statues.

Give each child some clay and let them shape it into anything they like. Set each creation on an index card with the child's name written on it.

ACTIVITY SEVEN: Human Bucket Chain Relay

Purpose

To move water from one end to the other by passing a bucket from child to child

Materials

- four large tubs (more for large groups)
- two buckets, small enough for children to manage (more for large groups)
- water

Preparation

Set two tubs at each end of the relay field and fill the ones at one end with water.

Procedure

Divide the children into two teams (or more if you have a lot of children), making sure that you have an even distribution of younger and older children.

Line them up on the field between the tubs.

Tell the children that the goal is to move the water from one tub to the other by filling the bucket with water and passing it from person to person.

When the bucket is emptied, the person at the end runs to the beginning of the chain and everyone moves down a bit. That person then dips the bucket in the water and hands it to the next person.

The relay is over when one of the tubs is empty. The winning team is the one with the most water in the second tub.

REGROUPING — STORY TIME

Book: *A Cool Drink of Water* by Barbara Kerley (Washington, D.C.: National Geographic Society, 2002)

FUN FACT: PURE WATER HAS NO SMELL AND NO TASTE.

WHOLE GROUP ACTIVITIES

ACTIVITY ONE: Discussing the Country of the Day—Ethiopia

Purpose

To locate Ethiopia on the map and discover its annual rainfall

Materials

- map of continents
- two labels marked Ethiopia
- tape
- four-inch blue yarn

Procedure

After story time, draw children's attention to the world map that was assembled during Lesson One. Remind them that they have been learning about rainfall in different countries around the world. Today, they will look at the country of Ethiopia.

Show them the Ethiopia label and ask if anyone knows where it belongs. If no one knows, call on a child to help you attach it to the proper place. Ask the children which continent Ethiopia is on (Africa). Tell them that the country is surrounded by other countries and is not next to the ocean.

Tell the children that today they are going to learn about a boy named Gamachu, who lives in Ethiopia. But first, would anyone like to guess how much rainfall Ethiopia gets in one year? Give the children a chance to guess and allow the one who guesses the closest to help you attach the yarn next to the previous strips. As you are attaching the yarn, tell the children that some parts of Ethiopia get only about four inches of rain each year.

ACTIVITY TWO: Comparing Our Lives

Purpose

To compare the children's daily lives with that of a boy who lives in Ethiopia

Materials

- adding machine tape
- marker
- plastic pitcher
- access to faucet
- paper towel tube
- rubber band
- stopwatch or clock with a second hand
- ruler or yardstick
- cookbook

Preparation

Measure a ten-yard strip of adding machine tape and wrap it around the paper towel tube. Secure with the rubber band.

Procedure

Using the photos from the book *Our World of Water,* talk with the children about Gamachu's daily life. Tell them that Gamachu lives in a part of Ethiopia that doesn't get much water. When water is hard to find, you have to spend much more of your day getting it.

Ask them, "What do you do for most of the day in the fall, winter, and spring?" (They go to school.) Tell the children that Gamachu doesn't go to school because it is his job to take the cattle to find food and water. When there hasn't been rain for a while, he might have to walk far to find the water.

The children may think it sounds great not to have to go to school, but help them realize how important school is. Tell them that one of the most important things they learn in school is how to read. We use reading for so many things, not just to read stories. (Show them the cookbook.)

For example, I have a cookbook here and it has recipes for how to make all kinds of yummy things. But if I can't read, I won't be able to figure out what to do. Ask the children if they can think of other times when it's important to be able to read. So even though school can be hard and there are times we'd rather be playing, going to school is important.

Gamachu spends a lot of time taking care of his family's cattle, but he does have some fun during the day. There are other children who take their families' cattle for water and they play together while the cattle eat and drink. Did anyone make animals from clay today? (Give time for response.) That is one of the ways Gamachu and his friends have fun—they make things out of clay. Did anyone play jacks? Gamachu and his friends play a game called toki, which is similar to our game of jacks. (See the photo on page 35 of *Our World of Water*.)

But if you don't have a lot of water, you have to do things differently. Ask the children how they brush their teeth. Do they know how to save water when they brush their teeth? (Turn the faucet off while brushing.) How would they be able to brush their teeth without water? (Give time for responses.) In Ethiopia, sometimes people may not brush with water, toothpaste, and a toothbrush at all. Gamachu uses sticks from special plants to clean his teeth. This way, he doesn't need water. (See the photo on page 35 of *Our World of Water*.) *Note:* Caution children not to try to brush their teeth with sticks because the sticks might damage their teeth or they might get sick from germs.

Tell the children that in Ethiopia, the rain comes at certain times of the year. During the rest of the year, it gets very dry. Ask the children what the relay was today. Tell them that sometimes where Gamachu lives, when it doesn't rain for a long time, the ponds near his home dry up. When that happens, he and his father have to take the animals far away to deeper wells. Other men come, too, to get water for their animals, and they form a human chain, just like the children did in the relay, to get the water from the deep well. (See the photo on page 37 of *Our World of Water*.)

Finally, select a child to take the pitcher to a faucet and fill about half full with water. Tell the child to walk at a normal pace and that you will time him or her to find out how long it takes to do this.

When the child returns with the water, tell the group how much time it took. Now, explain to them that you want to show that time on paper. You will do this by drawing a line. Every inch of line stands for one minute of time. For convenience, round the time to the nearest minute. For example, tell the children, "It took about three minutes to get this water. How long should my line be?" (Three inches) Measure and cut a strip of adding machine tape that is three inches long.

Now tell the children, "Where Gamachu lives in Ethiopia, his mother has to walk pretty far to get water from a pond. Can you guess how much time she spends each day getting water?" Let a couple of children unroll the adding machine tape that you have rolled on the paper towel tube. When they get it unrolled, tell them this represents the six hours that his mother walks every day to get water. Compare this strip to the small one you cut. Give the children time to respond to this.

As the leader, you will need to decide what your children are ready to understand. But an important point to make is that when clean water is not easy to get, people have to spend a lot of time trying to get water. This is time they can't spend going to school or doing other things that lead to a fulfilling life. One way we can help is by contributing to projects that work to provide clean water to these communities.

CLOSING

Reviewing

- What did you learn today about making dirty water clean?
- What things might we do, or not do, to help keep clean water from becoming dirty?
- What did you learn about Ethiopia that you didn't know?

PARTING PRAYER

O God: again we offer thanks for and we celebrate all forms of water on the earth. Help us to protect and keep clean all bodies of water—creeks, rivers, ponds, lakes, oceans, and wells. Amen.

Appendix

LETTERS TO PARENTS

LESSON ONE LETTER TO PARENTS

Dear Parents,

Thank you for sharing your child with us today. This week we will be focusing on the sacred gift of water and its importance to our world. Lessons will blend together Bible stories, facts about water, and information about how children in other parts of the world get and use water. Each day we'll send home a letter to let you know what we've done and to allow you the opportunity to continue at home the learning your child has begun.

The title of our lesson today was "Water in the Creation Story." Our scripture text was Genesis 1:1–2:4, and our verse of the day was "The Spirit of God was moving over the water" (Genesis 1:2 GNT). During the week you can continue to help your child develop familiarity of the Bible by looking up the scriptures together.

Here are some questions that you might discuss based on today's Bible studies:

1. What is the first thing on earth that is mentioned in the creation story? (water, raging ocean)

2. Why do you think it is so important that water is the first thing mentioned in the creation story? (All life on earth originated from water.)

3. When the waters came together so that the land appeared, what were the big bodies of water called? (seas)

4. Can you name something found in water that is vital to human life? (fish, for many people of the world their primary diet; salt)

5. Why is it so important that we celebrate and respect water? (Water is necessary for life; all life is dependent upon water.)

The big water fact we learned today was how much of the earth is covered with water. Ask your child how much that is. (It's 70 percent.) Was she or he surprised by that?

We began our discovery of how different countries get and use water by looking at our own town and how we use water in our daily lives. Does your child remember how much rainfall our town gets each year? If your child brought home a rain gauge, you can set it out the next time it rains.

You can also talk with your child about the small group activities. Here are some questions you might ask:

1. What happens when you put an egg in saltwater?

2. What happens when you put sugar in water? What about sand?

3. What continent do we live on?

4. Is it important for people to have clean water?

Or you could simply let your child share with you what he or she learned.

We would encourage you to continue exploring with your child the sacred gift of water. The public library has some good books, both fiction and nonfiction. Visit an aquarium. Or simply help your child notice the importance of water that surrounds them.

We look forward to seeing you tomorrow!

LESSON TWO LETTER TO PARENTS

Dear Parents,

The title of our lesson today was "Noah and the Flood." Our Scripture text was Genesis 6:9–9:16, and our focus of the day was "The rainbow is the sign of God's covenant." During the week you can continue to help your child develop familiarity of the Bible by looking up the scriptures together.

Here are some questions that you might discuss based on today's Bible studies:

1. Why do you think Noah was the one who built the ark? (He was a good man; he lived in fellowship with God; he was wise and able to see what was going on in the world.)

2. What was important about the animals that were taken onto the ark? (They were a male and female of each kind.)

3. Do you think the story about Noah is the only ancient story about a big flood? (No, many cultures have similar flood stories.)

4. Why was it important that the dove that Noah sent out came back with an olive branch in its mouth? (It meant there was life on the earth again.)

5. What was the sign of God's promise that the earth would never again be totally destroyed by water that we sometimes still see today? (The sign was a rainbow.)

The big water fact we learned today was the water cycle. Help your child recall the different stages of this cycle (evaporation, condensation, and precipitation). We also learned about the different states of water: solid (ice), liquid (water), and gas (water vapor).

We continued our discovery of how different countries get and use water by looking at a boy named Saran, who lives in Bangladesh. Perhaps your child can recall how often Saran takes a bath and how much water he uses. Ask your child if she or he made a flood-proof home and what she or he can tell you about it. What else can your child recall about Bangladesh?

You can also talk with your child about the small group activities. Here are some questions you might ask:

1. What kind of animal did you make for Noah's ark?

2. Did you make a clay ball float? How did you do it?

3. Did you build a levee? What does it do? (It blocks flood water.)

4. Are all clouds the same?

Or you could simply let your child share with you what he or she learned.
    We look forward to seeing you tomorrow!

Lesson Three Letter to Parents

Dear Parents,

The title of our lesson today was "Moses in the Basket on the Nile River." Our Scripture text was Exodus 1:8–10, 22; 2:1–10, and our focus of the day was "Water is God's sacred gift to the world."

Here are some questions that you might discuss based on today's Bible studies:

1. Why did the king of Egypt command that all the Hebrew baby boys be destroyed? (They feared the Hebrews would become so numerous they would rebel and cause trouble.)

2. What did Moses' mother do to try to save his life? (She put him in a basket and floated him down the river.)

3. Who found baby Moses in the basket? (The king's daughter found him.)

4. Who did the king's daughter pay to take care of baby Moses until he grew some? (She paid Moses' own mother.)

5. What did Moses grow up to become? (He became a great leader, the one who led his people out of slavery.)

The big water fact we learned today was that ice floats in water, which keeps marine life from dying in the cold winter. Ask your child what happened when we put a small ice cube in water. And what happened when we put a really big ice cube in water?

We continued our discovery of how different countries get and use water by looking at a boy named Lucas, who lives in Peru. Perhaps your child can recall where Lucas's water comes from (glaciers). Ask your child what it feels like to wash your hands in glacier water. What else can your child recall about Peru?

You can also talk with your child about the small group activities. Here are some questions you might ask:

1. Did you take the ice cube challenge? What happened to your ice cube?

2. Did you weave something today? Who wove something in the Bible story?

3. How do you keep a newspaper bowl from sinking?

4. Does a glacier move?

Or you could simply let your child share with you what he or she learned.

We look forward to seeing you tomorrow!

LESSON FOUR LETTER TO PARENTS

Dear Parents,

The title of our lesson today was "The Baptism of Jesus in the Jordan River." Our scripture text was Matthew 3:13–17, and our verse of the day was "As Jesus was baptized, he . . . saw the Spirit of God coming down like a dove and lighting on him" (Matthew 3:16, GNT). You can continue to help your child develop familiarity of the Bible by looking up the scriptures together.

Here are some questions that you might discuss based on today's Bible studies:

1. Have you seen someone—a baby, a child, or even an adult—be baptized?

2. What substance was used in the baptism? (water)

3. How was the water used? (sprinkled, poured, or otherwise)

4. Why do you think water is used in baptism? (Water is a universal symbol of washing, new beginning.)

5. Do you think the water used in baptism is changed in any way and becomes sacred, or is all water sacred?

The big water fact we learned today was that the smallest piece of water you can have is called a water molecule, which is made up of two hydrogen atoms and one oxygen atom. Did your child make a model of a water molecule? How did it look?

We continued our discovery of how different countries get and use water by looking at a girl named Barfimoh, who lives in Tajikistan. Does Barfimoh have running water in her house? (No) Where does her water come from? (From a spring at the bottom of a steep hill) What else can your child recall about Barfimoh and Tajikistan?

You can also talk with your child about the small group activities. Here are some questions you might ask:

1. Did you make a water wheel? How did it work?

2. What is water harvesting? Why do some people harvest water?

3. Did you build a dam? How did it work? Why do we build dams?

4. Did you make something with marshmallows?

Or you could simply let your child share with you what she or he learned.
    We look forward to seeing you tomorrow!

LESSON FIVE LETTER TO PARENTS

Dear Parents,

The title of our lesson today was "Jesus Stills the Waves." Our scripture text was Matthew 8:23–27, and our verse of the day was "[Jesus] ordered . . . the waves to stop, and there was a great calm" (Matthew 8:26, GNT).

Here are some questions that you might discuss based on today's Bible studies:

1. Have you ever ridden in a boat on a lake or ocean?

2. How would you feel if you were in a small boat on the lake when a storm arose and the waves started splashing water into the boat?

3. If you were in the boat during a storm, whom would you want in the boat with you? (someone strong who could bring the boat safely to the shore)

4. What can help us during those times when we are afraid? (faith, prayer, courage, remembering we are not alone)

5. Why do you think Jesus' followers have found courage to face frightening situations?

6. Could this story have meaning for us for all kinds of situations in our lives when we might be afraid?

The big water fact we learned today was that if you follow a water drop for one hundred years, it will spend less than one week in the atmosphere, twenty months as ice, about two weeks as freshwater, and about ninety-eight years in the ocean.

We continued our discovery of how diffcrent countries get and use water by looking at a girl named Khadija, who lives in Mauritania. Ask your child if Mauritania gets a lot of rain each year. (No) What are some things Khadija does to conserve water ? How do they keep water cool? (In clay pots) What else can your child recall about Khadija and Mauritania?

You can also talk with your child about the small group activities. Here are some questions you might ask:

1. Did you make waves today? Tell me about it.

2. What food is important to people who live near the ocean?

3. Did you make a sailboat? How well did it float?

4. Tell me how a submarine works.

Or you could simply let your child share with you what he or she learned.
We look forward to seeing you tomorrow!

LESSON SIX LETTER TO PARENTS

Dear Parents,

Today was the last day of our camp. We have enjoyed the time together and appreciate your helping your child be a part of our group.

The title of our final lesson was "Gathering at the Community Well." Our scripture text was taken from the Gospel of John, chapter 4, and our focus of the day was "Wells provide life-giving water."

Here are some questions that you might discuss based on today's Bible studies:

1. Have you ever seen a well?

2. Have you ever seen someone draw water from a well?

3. What do you think makes village wells so important? (Everyone depends on the water the well provides; the well can be a village gathering place.)

4. Why is it so important to protect the community well? (The water needs to be kept clean, pure, and free of contamination.)

5. What might we do to help a community or village have a well or clean drinking water? (Collect money for digging a well or collect money for clean water filters.)

The big water fact we learned today was how much water on the earth is available for us (and other living things) to use. Ask your child what they thought about this. Were they surprised at how little water is available? (1 percent)

We continued our discovery of how different countries get and use water by looking at a boy named Gamachu, who lives in Ethiopia. Does Gamachu go to school? Why not? What is Gamachu's task? (to take the family animals to find water) How much time does his mother spend each day getting water for the family? (six hours) What else can your child recall about Ethiopia?

You can also talk with your child about the small group activities. Here are some questions you might ask:

1. Can you tell me a way to make dirty water clean?

2. What does Gamachu do for fun?

3. What is a human bucket chain? Why would you use one?

4. Where does well water come from?

Or you could simply let your child share with you what he or she learned.

Thank you for sharing your child(ren) with us this past week as we have studied, explored, and celebrated the sacred gift of water!

Resource List

CHAPTER ONE

Good News Bible(s).

Graham, Joan Bransfield. *Splish, Splash.* Illustrated by Steve Scott. New York: Tickner & Fields, 1994.

Hollyer, Beatrice. *Our World of Water: Children and Water Around the Word.* New York: Henry Holt, 2009.

"Itsy, Bitsy Spider" music, traditional; Roud Folk Song Index #11586.

The New Century Hymnal. Cleveland: Pilgrim Press, 1995.

CHAPTER TWO

De Paola, Tomie. *The Cloud Book.* New York: Holiday House, 1975.

Good News Bible(s).

Hollyer, Beatrice. *Our World of Water: Children and Water Around the Word.* New York: Henry Holt, 2009.

"Itsy, Bitsy Spider" music, traditional; Roud Folk Song Index #11586.

The New Century Hymnal. Cleveland: Pilgrim Press, 1995.

Wells, Robert E. *Did a Dinosaur Drink This Water?* Park Ridge, IL: Albert Whitman, 2006.

CHAPTER THREE

Cassino, Mark. With Jon Nelson, Ph.D. *The Story of Snow: The Science of Winter's Wonder.* San Francisco: Chronicle Books, 2009.

Good News Bible(s).

Hollyer, Beatrice. *Our World of Water: Children and Water Around the Word.* New York: Henry Holt, 2009.

"Itsy, Bitsy Spider" music, traditional; Roud Folk Song Index #11586.

The New Century Hymnal. Cleveland: Pilgrim Press, 1995.

CHAPTER FOUR

Gonzalez, Maya Christina. *I Know the River Loves Me.* San Francisco: Children's Book Press, 2009.

Good News Bible(s).

Hollyer, Beatrice. *Our World of Water: Children and Water Around the Word.* New York: Henry Holt, 2009.

"Itsy, Bitsy Spider" music, traditional; Roud Folk Song Index #11586.

The New Century Hymnal. Cleveland: Pilgrim Press, 1995.

Stone, Lynn M. *How Are They Built? Dams.* Vero Beach, FL: Rourke, 2002.

CHAPTER FIVE

Good News Bible(s).

Hollyer, Beatrice. *Our World of Water: Children and Water Around the Word.* New York: Henry Holt, 2009.

Hooper, Meredith. Illustrated by Bee Willey. *River Story.* Cambridge, MA: Candlewick Press, 2000.

"Itsy, Bitsy Spider" music, traditional; Roud Folk Song Index #11586.

The New Century Hymnal. Cleveland: Pilgrim Press, 1995.

CHAPTER SIX

Good News Bible(s).

Hollyer, Beatrice. *Our World of Water: Children and Water Around the Word.* New York: Henry Holt, 2009.

"Itsy, Bitsy Spider" music, traditional; Roud Folk Song Index #11586.

Kerley, Barbara. *A Cool Drink of Water.* Washington, D.C.: National Geographic Society, 2002.

The New Century Hymnal. Cleveland: Pilgrim Press, 1995.

OTHER BOOKS FROM RANDY HAMMER

WHAT'S SO AMAZING ABOUT POLAR BEARS?
Teaching Kids to Care for Creation

RANDY HAMMER, KRISTIN HAMMER EVANS & SUZANNE BLOKLAND

ISBN 978-0-8298-1877-2/paper/144 pages/$14

This is an ideal resource for elementary school–aged children. Each lesson has an ecology theme with a scriptural background for study, reflection, and discussion; fun facts relevant to the topic; experiential activities to engage the children and reinforce the lesson; and much, much more. Children will learn while having fun exploring ways to care for God's precious creation—earth and its inhabitants.

52 WAYS TO IGNITE YOUR CONGREGATION
Practical Hospitality

RANDY HAMMER

ISBN 978-0-8298-1825-3/paper/96 pages/$14

This book is a practical and timely resource for clergy and laity. It offers fifty-two short (one- to two-page) practical pointers to assist congregations in extending hospitality to newcomers, making them feel welcome, and taking positive steps to ensure they look forward to returning.

THE SINGING BOWL
26 Children's Sermons with Activities

RANDY HAMMER

ISBN 978-0-8298-1851-2/paper/96 pages/$14

With a scripture passage, object for sharing, suggestions for presentation and follow-up, and hands-on activities and experiences, each of Hammer's twenty-six original and imaginative sermons in *The Singing Bowl* follow the order of the church and liturgical year with a progressive Christian perspective that places an emphasis on respecting the dignity and individuality of each child.

THE SHINING LIGHT
26 Children's Sermons with Activities

RANDY HAMMER

ISBN 978-0-8298-1868-0/paper/96 pages/$16

The Shining Light is a collection of positive, original stories and lessons, with activities for clergy and lay leaders to use in preaching to children from kindergarten through upper-elementary school. The topics generally follow the church year beginning in September and ending with Pentecost.

THE TALKING STICK
40 Children's Sermons with Activities

RANDY HAMMER

ISBN 978-0-8298-1761-4/paper/96 pages/$15

The Talking Stick is a collection of children's stories or lessons whose topics generally follow the church year beginning in September and ending with Pentecost. An overall aim throughout the stories is to lift up the divine image that is planted within each child in order to promote equality, justice, and the inherent worth and dignity of all children. Additionally, it encourages each child to be the best he or she was created to be.

To order these or any other books from The Pilgrim Press call or write to:

THE PILGRIM PRESS
700 PROSPECT AVENUE EAST
CLEVELAND, OHIO 44115-1100

PHONE ORDERS: 1-800-537-3394 ■ FAX ORDERS: 216-736-2206

Please include shipping charges of $7.00 for the first book and $1.00 for each additional book. Or order from our web sites at www.thepilgrimpress.com and www.uccresources.com.

Prices subject to change without notice.